PENGUIN BOOKS

HOW TO BE WEIRD

Eric G. Wilson is the author of *Against Happiness*,
Everyone Loves a Good Train Wreck, and *Keep It
Fake*. He lives in Winston-Salem, North Carolina.

ALSO BY ERIC G. WILSON

Against Happiness: In Praise of Melancholy

Everyone Loves a Good Train Wreck: Why We Can't Look Away

Keep It Fake: Inventing an Authentic Life

HOW TO BE WEIRD

AN OFF-KILTER GUIDE
TO LIVING A
ONE-OF-A-KIND LIFE

Eric G. Wilson

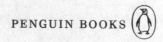

PENGUIN BOOKS

PENGUIN BOOKS

An imprint of Penguin Random House LLC
penguinrandomhouse.com

Quote by Claudia Rankine, page 1; Quote by Susan Griffin, page 5; Quote by Marshall
McLuhan, page 19; Quote by Rebecca Solnit, page 21; Quote by Samuel Taylor Coleridge, page
26; Quote by Rita Dove, page 30; Quote by Anne Carson, page 34; Quote by Vladimir Nabokov,
page 36; Quote by Virginia Woolf, page 49; Quote by Toni Morrison, page 51; Quote by
Jean Baudrillard, page 56; Quote by Eileen Myles, page 61; Quote by Sharon Dolin, page 63;
Quote by Colson Whitehead, page 66; Quote by Heinrich von Kleist, page 71; Quote by
Tao Lin, page 80; Quote by Carlos Fuentes, page 92; Quote by Salman Rushdie, page 96;
Quote by Cynthia Ozick, page 108; Quote by Mike Birbiglia, page 114; Quote by Jericho Brown,
page 127; Quote by James Dickey, page 132; Quote by John Cage, page 134; Quote by
Maxine Hong Kingston, page 137; Quote by Anaïs Nin, page 139; Quote by W. G. Sebald,
page 142; Quote by A. R. Ammons, page 145; Quote by William Shakespeare, page 150;
Quote by Derek Walcott, page 152; Quote by Junot Díaz, page 154; Quote by Ross Gay,
page 156; Quote by Walt Whitman, page 159; Quote by Walter Benjamin, page 165;
Quote by Octavio Paz, page 178; Quote by Emily Dickinson, page 180

LIBRARY OF CONGRESS CATALOGING-IN-PUBLICATION DATA
Names: Wilson, Eric G., 1967– author.
Title: How to be weird : an off-kilter guide to living a one-of-a-kind life / Eric G. Wilson.
Identifiers: LCCN 2021051095 (print) | LCCN 2021051096 (ebook) |
ISBN 9780143136576 (trade paperback) | ISBN 9780525508076 (ebook)
Subjects: LCSH: Personality and creative ability. | Eccentrics and eccentricities. |
Self-actualization (Psychology)
Classification: LCC BF698.9.C74 W55 2022 (print) |
LCC BF698.9.C74 (ebook) | DDC 153.3/5—dc23/eng/20211214
LC record available at https://lccn.loc.gov/2021051095
LC ebook record available at https://lccn.loc.gov/2021051096

Printed in the United States of America
1st Printing

Set in Ysobel Pro • Designed by Sabrina Bowers

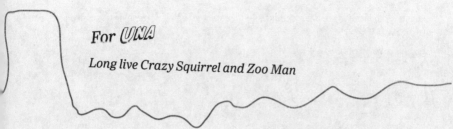

For *UNA*

Long live Crazy Squirrel and Zoo Man

We're all misfits here. . . . From our weirdnesses and our differences, from our manic fixations, our obsessions, our passions. From all those wild and wacky things that make each of us unique.

TERRI WINDLING

The freak becomes the great unifier. The alien is the best company after all . . .

TILDA SWINTON

I'm gonna wave my freak flag high.

JIMI HENDRIX

Contents

Introduction

"*D*o you feel weird? I feel weird."

"Yeah, I feel a little weird. Do you really feel weird?"

"I *definitely* feel weird."

So goes a regular tongue-in-cheek dialogue between myself and my sixteen-year-old daughter. We perform it as opportunities arise, perhaps during an awkward pause in a conversation about bunting, or at the close of a spooky Kate Bush song, or after a deadpan scene in a Jim Jarmusch film, or after we've read an evangelical bumper sticker on the black pickup truck in front of us at a stoplight: "My God's Last Name Isn't Damn!"

It all started with far-out games we'd play when she was a little girl. Who's Crying in the Closet? The Superfluous Professor! Barbie Brunches at the Crazy Zoo! In the thick of the playing, I would pause, raise my right eyebrow, and ask, in my best Dr. Freud voice, if she felt weird.

"Yes! Again! Again!"

A few weeks ago, my fiancée asked why my daughter and I staged this shtick.

"Because life is boring."

*W*eirdness: Is it not essential to a compelling life?

You doze while watching *Donnie Darko* on your laptop and you slip into a dream of your daughter singing, but she sounds like Jake Gyllenhaal. You jolt awake in wonderment.

During a hike you bound up boulders and find yourself on a cliff. You hear a voice to your right, turn, and there is a person in blue, and you have that sensation: this has happened *before*. Time is no longer a line but a spiral.

Go to a wax museum, primed for the campiness. But you look too long at Lorde. Was that a wink?

These feelings of thrilling unease—not beauty, truth, or goodness—are what draw us to the museum, poetry, the art film, the alt music club. Study Basquiat's *King Alphonso* or read Emily Dickinson's "There's a certain Slant of light" or watch Jordan Peele's *Us* or listen to Lana Del Rey's "Video Games." For a breath, the world bends and then snaps back and all is new.

We crave the weird—the quirky, the eccentric, the peculiar, the freaky, the far-out—because it estranges us from our normal habits of thought and perception, nullifies old conceptual maps, and so propels us into uncharted regions, outlandish and bracing, where we must create, if we are to thrive, coordinates more capacious than the ones we already know.

*T*hink of all the strange moments that inspirit us: not only déjà vu and the uncanniness of waxworks and the limbo between wakefulness and sleep, but also getting lost and returning repeatedly to the same spot, bumping into your double, the recurrence of the same number multiple times in one day, sensing the presence of a deceased relative, omens, signs, entering a dark basement, low-grade fevers, wandering through an unfamiliar city at twilight, vertigo, a solitary crow cawing in a winter field.

Great creators have made the outré their oeuvre. The "eccentric artist" is a cliché, but not an inaccurate one. Truman Capote feared planes with two nuns on board and avoided rooms containing yellow roses. Estée Lauder touched the faces of random strangers. Monkeys, peacocks, a bear, a crane, and a crocodile were the pets of Lord Byron, who imbibed wine from skulls. Frida Kahlo also enjoyed a menagerie, including a fawn named Granizo and an eagle called Gertrudis Caca Blanca, or White Shit Gertrude. Charles Dickens stuffed the paw of his dead cat Bob and affixed it to an ivory letter opener. Poet Gérard de Nerval walked a lobster on a leash. Einstein gathered cigarette butts and smoked them in his pipe. Enamored of oxidization, Dalí peed on the brass bands of fountain pens. Shirley Jackson, author of "The Lottery," practiced witchcraft. To finish *The Hunchback of Notre Dame* on time, Victor Hugo locked himself in his room naked. Nineteenth-century poet Friedrich Schiller stored rotten apples in his desk and inhaled them as he wrote. French composer Erik Satie consumed only white food and collected umbrellas. Steve Jobs ate so many carrots his skin turned orange. Buckminster Fuller, architect of the geodesic dome, wore three watches, slept only two hours in a day, and updated his diary every fifteen minutes. Maya Angelou wrote best in hotel rooms, from 6:30 a.m. to 1:30 p.m.; she required that the sheets never be cleaned and that sherry, playing cards, and a Bible always be on hand. Yayoi Kusama, artist of infinite mirrors, chooses to live in an asylum and paint her world in polka dots. Tilda Swinton sleeps in glass boxes in the middle of museums. Björk crawls to rehearsals from her apartment.

Geniuses tend to be weird because they embrace those parts of themselves that separate them from the masses—parts unprecedented, unpredictable, unrepeatable.

If you crave originality, cultivate the strange. This is not easy.

Go singular, and you risk being misunderstood, feared, disliked, ignored. But without this gamble, how will you spark your flair?

How to Be Weird is a guidebook for how to be you, which means becoming hyperalert to those curious oscillations only you can sense because you are *this* person at *this* place at *this* time. Jibe with these currents, swirl them.

This "weird" is not "W.E.I.R.D," the acronym researchers use to describe the relatively small group—an eighth of the world's population—that makes up 60 to 90 percent of the participants in psychological studies: people who are White, Educated, Industrialized, Rich, and Democratic. Far from pertaining only to comfortable white people, weirdness as I see it challenges homogenization and conformity, and it valorizes particularity and otherness.

Weirdness is therefore political. Through irony, satire, silliness, hyperbole, reverie, and dream, it questions the status quo and liberates new possibilities. Groups that have viewed weirdness this way are the Dadaists, the French Surrealists, the Chicago Surrealist Group, the Négritude movement, and the Afro-Surrealists.

The exercises that follow will help you release your inner weird. They require nothing fancy in the way of tools and technology, nor are they overly taxing. All you need is a little play in your schedule and the following:

A notebook

(This is the most important tool for your venture, since many of the exercises invite you to record observations, emotions, lists, or definitions. What kind of notebook? The choices seem endless. You can pick color, size [letter, half-letter, pocket-sized], binding [spiral, stitched, glued], cover [hard, soft], weight of paper, number of pages, style of pages [blank, ruled, or gridded], and price [from the twenty dollar Moleskine to the fifty cent Composition]. Here's some guidance: one hundred years from now, when your ancestors are searching through your final belongings and they find an old liquor-store box labeled *WEIRD NOTEBOOKS* and they open it, what do you want them to see first?)

A pencil or pen

(This choice is almost as important as your notebook. If the paper is a space inspiring your traverse, your writing implement is your vehicle. The old No. 2 Ticonderoga is iconic and serviceable, but you've got to keep up with a small sharpener. Mechanical pencils are sleek and promise a clear line; those lead sticks break so easily, though. Pens, from fountain to ballpoint, are less hassle. They can stain and bleed, however, and sometimes you want to erase What decides it? If the pencil or pen feels good in your hand, like your old tennis racket, knitting needles, drumsticks, chopping knife, or artist's paintbrush, then that's the one.)

Art paper

(9 x 12 or 11 x 14 in a ring-bound sketchbook is probably best, but loose copy paper will do.)

Colored pencils or markers

A paintbrush and watercolors

Play-Doh or modelling clay

All-purpose glue

A camera (a smartphone camera is fine)

A voice recorder (a voice-recording app in a smartphone works)

Decent walking shoes

You can work through the exercises in order—they loosely follow one year's seasons, from summer to spring—or you can skip around to suit your fancy.

And there is no need to complete all the exercises. Or any of them. Just imagining how you would approach an activity will swerve your mind temporarily from its grooves. But actually breaking off a witching stick or making ink from pennies or coloring your own Tarot deck might knock you clear out of your rut.

If this book doesn't cultivate creativity, self-knowledge, and empathy—as I hope it will—at least it will distract you, and since boredom is, according to Kierkegaard, the "despairing refusal to be oneself," it is good to be distracted.

It is better, though, to be enchanted.

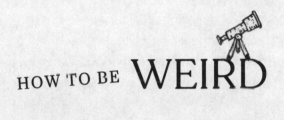

HOW TO BE WEIRD

1.

Create an Overview Effect

The sky shivers
in puddles created of night rain.

CLAUDIA RANKINE

*W*hen Apollo 14 astronaut Edgar Mitchell first saw Earth from the Moon, he arose to a euphoric "global consciousness." Psychologist Frank White calls this sudden expansion from creature to creation the "overview effect": the feeling of awe upon realizing "how small the Earth is in the scheme of things." This "Universal Insight" inspires "a sense of the unity of everything in the universe and an understanding that our ultimate destiny is to become citizens of the universe."

When he returned to earth, Mitchell quit NASA to form the Institute of Noetic Sciences, which is devoted to exploring interconnectivity and recently developed a virtual reality version of Mitchell's lunar epiphany. Mitchell is not alone in his earthly proselytizing. The overview effect converted Jim Irwin, of Apollo 15, into an evangelist, and Al Worden, of the same mission, into a poet. Apollo 16's Charlie Duke turned into a born-again Christian.

You don't need to go moony to explode your skull.

Lie on your stomach.

For five minutes, study the ground ten inches from your face.

Light on a blade of grass, a weed you don't know, clover, moss texture, moss color, dampness or dryness, an acorn maybe or a tiny flower, dirt, sand, pine needle, leaf, little exoskeletons, little snail shells.

Roll over and open to the sky.

Imagine you are floating up there, cloud-high, and you behold yourself below, and you lock eyes with yourself.

Remain on your back for about five minutes, wondering what your heavenly self thinks about your earthly one.

Roll back over, recover an object from the small plot that launched you skyward in the first place. Take your souvenir—a tuft of moss, maybe—and place it in a glass beside your bed.

Next time you feel anxious or bitter, study your memento and remember that you are only a perception away from synching with the firmament. From aloft, your worries are small, your heart immense.

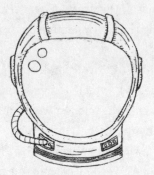

2.

Encourage
Moments of Yūgen

Alan Watts, one of the first to explain Buddhist aesthetics to Western audiences, admired the Zen concept of yūgen, often translated into English as a feeling of mysterious profundity. But as Watts explains in his lecture "The Way of Tea," this definition misses the subtlety of the sensation, best rendered through images. You experience yūgen watching the sun sink beyond a hill covered in poppies, or witnessing wild geese disappear into a bank of clouds, or walking on a strange path—an old mining road, an abandoned railroad track, a shaded walkway in a city park—with no thought of returning.

These encounters, evocative blends of alertness and longing, are rare, Watts believes, because our perception is usually controlled by two drives: to survive and to understand. In survival mode, we see only what meets our most basic needs; in pursuit of comprehension, we notice only what conforms to our mental frameworks.

But then, sudden as weather: those moments—inscrutable but exhilarating—that silence our practical concerns and call us to unexplored regions over the knoll, behind the wall, on the other side of that door.

This is the essence of yūgen: there is always a beyond, and beyond that, another beyond, and beyond that, another, and so on, forever. Doors open to doors, deeps to deeps. "Enough" is illusion; "more," only, is real.

Foster your own moments of yūgen.

Set aside an hour at dawn or twilight.

Take a solitary walk. As you move, recall the thrilling anticipations of your childhood. Anything could happen!

Now pay attention to thresholds along your way: doors, gates, fences, windows, manholes, tree hollows, hills, clouds, puddles, fountains.

What's on the other side? Let your mind play among possibilities, the stranger the better.

When you get home, on a single sheet of paper, write one sentence or draw a small image that represents this walk. Store the page in a drawer or under your mattress or in the pages of a book or in a jewelry box.

If you feel frayed and tired, take out the page and remember, there is *something else.*

3.

Astonish Your Words

*I love that moment in writing when I know language
falls short. There is something more there.*

SUSAN GRIFFIN

In his memoir *Darkness Visible* (1990), William Styron laments the word "depression." It is "a noun with a bland tonality and lacking any magisterial presence. . . . Nonetheless for over seventy-five years the word has slithered innocuously through the language like a slug, leaving little trace of its intrinsic malevolence and preventing, by its very insipidity, a general awareness of the horrible intensity of the disease when out of control."

But aren't all words for intense feelings deficient? "I'm in love" ridiculously misses the crazed vulnerability. To be "anxious" is oceans away from the nauseating flutters and lethal-seeming suffocation. We crave expressions closer to the bone.

Poets press their words nearer to experience by redefining them imagistically.

Emily Dickinson's depression is a "Funeral, in [her] Brain."

Death for E. E. Cummings is "no parenthesis."

Life for Langston Hughes "ain't been no crystal stair."

Love for Charles Bukowski: "a dog from hell."

You, too, can liberate your words from the lexicon.

What word best describes your current mood? Write it at the top of a page, followed by "is." Now come up with three strikingly concrete definitions that propel the word closer to your feelings.

If your mood is petulance, for instance, you might write the following.

Petulance is:

(1) A sparrow with no branch to land on

(2) A shell shard the surf flings into the sand

(3) A single tree in a field bent by wind

Once you have reanimated your word, you are likely more intimate with your mood. It is now not just a sensation, like fever or a chill. It is a thing. You can hold it and stare at it and keep it near you. Or you can put it down and walk away.

4.

Turn This Book
into a Shovel

M. C. Escher asked, "Are you sure that a floor cannot also be a ceiling?" Marcel Duchamp turned a urinal into a fountain. Look at a drawing of a duck's head, watch it shift into the noggin of a rabbit, and regret (well, maybe) that you didn't major in philosophy.

Things are as tired of being themselves as we are.

Liberate objects from their traditional uses, and thrill to the enchantment: you can turn anything into virtually anything.

Start small. Take a paper clip. What else can you bend it into? A hook or, perhaps, a key ring, or an un-clogger of glue containers, or the letter "L," or the letter "O," or a bracelet, or a thin metallic worm.

Then there is this story, reported by Francis H. Cook in his translation of Dōgen, *Sounds of Valley Streams*: "A Zen master pointed to a fan and asked two monks what it was. The first monk picked it up and fanned himself silently. . . . The other monk took the fan, placed a tea cake on it, and offered it to the master. The 'fan' was now a serving tray. This is the emptiness of the fan." This means there is no such thing as "fan-ness," just as there is no such thing as "paper-clip-ness." These are just ghostly concepts that attempt to fix an object onto one meaning. But in reality a thing is less a noun and more a verb, not so much a solid as a likelihood.

Practice, right now, turning element to energy.

Close this book. What can you make it? Maybe a tray, a plinth, a rectangular fluttering frisbee, a weapon, a shovel that works only in the loosest of sand, something to try to spin on your index finger, something to barter for something better, a tiny platform that makes you a little taller, a plate for potato chips, a triangle or a dollhouse (if you open it slightly and stand it on the longer edges of the cover), a measure of your posture or a mortarboard (if you balance it on your head), an example of a rectangle, a potential shade, a falling object, a thing to toss.

Now find your own object and do your magic.

Scientists say such transmogrifying will improve your creativity. It will also soften your facts into fantasies.

Who doesn't want that?

5.

Go Sinister

*P*hilosopher Charles Sanders Peirce—neuralgic, impoverished, criminal, morphine addicted, subsisting on stale bread, creator of pragmatism, owner of a 2,000-acre estate called "Arisbe" (possibly an anagram of the French "baiser," to kiss)—was a lefty. He believed this sinister-handedness had caused his woes, and so he grew dexterous with his right. He astounded students by writing questions with his left hand while simultaneously answering them with his right.

Peirce's intuition about left-handedness and angst has proven accurate: southpaws are more likely than righties to have mental illness. But he was probably wrong about a hand's ability to influence the brain. (He lived from 1839 to 1914, before the computer-enhanced sophistication of modern neurology.) As far as scientists know, you can't strengthen one side of the brain by developing the opposing hand. And even if you could invigorate a mental hemisphere, relief from clinical depression would likely not result.

But we should still learn to write with our nondominant hands.

Have you ever said, "forth and back" instead of "back and forth"? Have you ever imagined, while driving, that your car is still and the landscape moves? Have you ever stared out your window at a house across the street and envisioned how you must look to the person living in the house, gazing out of her own window?

In each instance, your habitual perspective turns into its opposite. Worthy of Lewis Carroll's Wonderland, such sudden cognitive reversals are vertiginous but also salubrious. In encompassing contradiction, they encourage us to be more tolerant, empathetic, generous, comfortable with ambiguity, and wary of oversimplification.

To learn to write with your nondominant hand is to entertain these virtues.

At the beginning of each day, write your name in your opposite hand. Concentrate on the awkward transition from same to different.

Eventually, you might graduate to other words, to sentences, to paragraphs, to a full other-handed alter ego.

6.

Assemble a Shadow Box

Joseph Cornell believed that "complete happiness" was "quickly being plunged into a world in which every triviality becomes imbued with significance." He reached this joy with his art. When he could escape his cramped house in Queens, where he lived all his adult life with his mother and disabled brother, Cornell haunted Manhattan's antique stores, thrift shops, five-and-dimes, used bookstores, and old print shops. He acquired soap bubble pipes, children's blocks, dolls, marbles, cordial glasses, rings, fake ice cubes (made of glass), thimbles, string, prints of ballerinas, images of Hollywood starlets, passages cut from astronomy books, pictures of birds and shells, and all other manner of bric-a-brac. From his collection he harvested the most captivating objects, and he arranged them in wooden boxes. In these miniature theaters the striking juxtapositions made the things move and live.

One "shadow box," called *Bébé Marie*, features a female Victorian doll standing within twigs painted silver—a modern fairy tale, innocence imprisoned in the magical forest. Another, *Medici Slot Machine*, displays a picture of a Medici boy prince whose hauteur contrasts with whimsical blocks and marbles below; two clock springs among the toys suggest the spiraling nature of time—young boys always wish to be old, old men long for their youth. In yet another of Cornell's poetic theaters, *Aviary with Parrot and Drawers*, a cutout of a parrot perches in a vertically rectangular space in the midst of a small chest of drawers; loosely coiled clock springs are attached to a white background just behind the bird's head. This is the artist cramped by space and time.

You flip through a magazine, and a picture of a parakeet is simply that, and you keep flipping. Same with an acorn in your driveway, or that odd piece of metal you found in your basement. But when you place one of these things in a box, painted blue or covered in velvet, and throw in whatever else seems to fit, then you have sacralized the object. You have elevated it from ordinary to extraordinary.

Make your own Cornell box.

First, spend a week gathering odds and ends that stimulate your imagination.

Choose seven things from your collection.

Take a shoebox and color the inside of it a hue suitable to your objects. If you would like, glue fabric or interesting cutouts into the space.

Within the box, arrange your seven objects into an interesting pattern. Secure all or some with glue or tape, according to your vision.

Display your miniature theater. Note how its meaning shifts over the weeks, as your mind creates fresh analogies among the objects.

Create a box for every season of the year.

7.

Arrange a Wunderkammer

*A*thanasius Kircher, a German Jesuit who taught at the Roman College during the seventeenth century, was a dazzling polymath. He distinguished himself as a linguist (he discovered a link between the Coptic and Egyptian languages), historian (he wrote an encyclopedia of China), geologist (he studied volcanoes and fossils), physician (he hypothesized infectious microorganisms as the cause of the plague), inventor (he created a magnetic clock), and biblical scholar (he analyzed the distribution of Noah's animals).

Kircher also curated his famous Wunderkammer, or Room of Wonders. In this cabinet of curiosities were objects reflecting his eclectic interests, including Egyptian obelisks, mastodon bones, stones from India thought to draw out snake venom, magic lanterns, an organ playing birdsongs, a statue of an eagle that could vomit, and a configuration of mirrors that could reveal ghosts. Kircher fashioned a tube leading from the exhibitions to his bedroom; through it, he could listen to his visitors' comments and answer their questions.

If Kircher's Wunderkammer could be guilty of exoticizing non-Western cultures (his well-traveled Jesuit brothers donated artifacts from Africa, India, China, and Japan), a more recent Wonder Room respects cultural differences. In her installation *New World Wunderkammer*, on display from 2013 to 2014, Chicana artist Amalia Mesa-Bains created curiosity cabinets devoted to Africa, America's indigenous peoples, and the New World's intricate blending of race and culture. Drawing from her own collection and the collection at UCLA's Fowler Museum, Mesa-Bains organized objects under the categories of "memory, struggle, loss, and wonder." This classification challenged traditional European arrangements based on scientific concepts and the whims of the collector. Included in Mesa-Bain's collection were artifacts of "war, religion, and culture" as well as digital prints of lost objects. Mesa-Bains wanted these images to "heal . . . loss and displacement."

Make your own Wunderkammer. Set aside a space in your dwelling—could be one shelf, a corner, an entire room—and install there any objects that you find interesting and odd. You might display objects you already possess. A favorite old book, for instance, or a worn playing card, or that cicada shell your daughter found.

Once you have a basic idea of your quirks, your eyes—like magnets—will seek out things that suit your energy. These can be objects you find lying around your house or out in your neighborhood. They can be things you acquire in antique and thrift stores, or artifacts from obscure travels, or things handed down by your family.

Perhaps you will find over time that these objects reflect more than your personal inclinations. Do they represent your family's history, or the concerns of a social or ethnic group of which you are a part? What is the abiding emotion to the collection? Joy? Sadness?

Regardless of the collection's mood, your search for oddities has made you more alert to the world. You are always on the lookout for something strange. When you find it, you grasp more than the object; you hold a piece of your heart.

8.

Design a Mappa Mundi

*T*he charm of an ancient map is that it's not a map, thanks to its woefully inadequate geography. But if it can't get you where you want to go physically, it can direct you to realms of imaginative splendor: monster-teeming oceans, cities domed in gold, phantasmal geometries. This is cartography as art, and its wonders are those of sci-fi and fantasy.

Like novels, very old maps reveal the dreams of their makers. They are confessions made of space.

Take an Islamic world map from 1154, part of al-Sharīf al-Idrīsī's *The Entertainment for He Who Longs to Travel the World*, commissioned by the king of Sicily. Unlike the many mapmakers of old who relied on reading and speculation, al-Sharīf al-Idrīsī actually interviewed travelers from around the world, from as far away as China and Norway. At the beginning of the book—composed of seventy regional maps—is a circular map of the world. Fire forms the circumference, as the Koran envisions, and the flames surround a second circle of blue: the sea. At the top of the circumscribed landmasses, Arabia at their center, is the south, a typical orientation in Islamic maps. Early Muslims lived just north of

Mecca, the Holy City, and so believed that south was the direction of prayer, and thus the superior coordinate. Like Arabia, Africa is prominent, while Europe, an oversized Sicily notwithstanding, is vague by comparison.

Where al-Sharīf al-Idrīsī's map reflects Islam and empiricism, the anonymous maker of the Hereford Mappa Mundi (c. 1300) expresses fancy and Christianity. The map follows a common European design of the time, the "T and O," a circle divided into three sections by a "T": Asia, the circle's top hemisphere, which points east; Europe, the bottom hemisphere's left, or northern, half; and Africa, the southerly right half. Eden, to which all Christians aspire, rests at the circle's top, while Jerusalem, God's proxy, stands in the center. Above Jerusalem is Babylon, signaling pride; below is Rome, spiritual guide to the fallen world. On the margins to the left and right are monsters:  the Essedones, who gobble up their parents; the Sciapods, whose one giant foot shades them; the Phanesii, large ears engulfing their bodies; and the Gangines, whom the scent of apples nourishes.

Draw your own mental map.

First form a circle.

At its apex, depict, in words or images, the state of being you most hanker for. In the circle's center, represent the part of you that best reflects this ideal.

Now fill in the spaces as your identity dictates.

Do you feel defensive? Then perhaps sketch a ring of fire.

Are you anxious or depressed? Then where do your monsters lurk? On the margins? Near the center?

Maybe you face obstacles. What stands between your core and acme?

Are you sanguine? Cluster your symbols near the top.

When you are finished, color the map with paints or markers. Hang it on your refrigerator. It will remind you of your flaws and inspire your talents.

9.

Forge a New Identity

The name of a man is a numbing blow from which he never recovers.

MARSHALL MCLUHAN

Mary Anne Evans settled on "George Eliot" when women novelists were undervalued. "George Orwell" suited Eric Blair, a "good round English name" that also hid his authorship of a book he was ashamed of, *Down and Out in Paris and London*. A new name fell onto Samuel Langhorne Clemens after his habit of striding into a Virginia City bar and booming out "Mark Twain!" This was the riverboat phrase—meaning the vessel at two fathoms—he used to order his two whiskies, which the barkeep tallied on the wall with two chalk marks.

Paramount found "Archibald Leach" infelicitous, and so gave their new British performer a list of sturdy American monikers. He picked "Cary Grant." Her talent for farting and belief that a Jewish name would help her in Hollywood inspired Caryn Elaine Johnson to morph into Whoopi Goldberg.

These famous people changed their names for a variety of

reasons: to get published, to hide something, to celebrate gusto, to achieve euphony, to land roles while cutting the mustard.

But were there deeper reasons for the fresh monikers? Recent research has shown that a person's name can significantly shape their personality, maybe even their face. Names come with built-in expectations—people assume a "Bob" will have a rounder face than a "Tim," for instance, and a "Katherine" will be more success-ful than a "Scarlett"—and we might find ourselves unconsciously striving to meet these standards. We can do this through our cloth-ing, hair, speech, mannerisms, and expressions. Over time, our face might shape itself to fit the name's requirements. We *become* the character our name determines.

Did the celebrities mentioned above feel too constrained by their given names? Did they desire a new role, one they could play more successfully?

What about you? Would you like to change your name, your nar-rative? Or, less grandiosely, are you simply weary of what people have been calling you all these years? Is your name too common? Too difficult to pronounce? Not dignified enough, or too pompous?

Whatever the reason, and even if you kind of like your present one, create another name for yourself, first and last. Add a middle if you'd like.

Attach a brief biography to this name. What can this person do that you can't?

Once you create your new identity, write the name on a piece of paper, fold it up, put it in your purse or wallet.

Whenever someone insults you, or you feel insecure, or are just weary of being you, take out your alternative appellation, imagine being that person, and feel a little relief before returning to—as you must—your old ego, not so bad after all.

10.

Pursue Astral Pareidolia

The stars we are given. The constellations we make.
That is to say, stars exist in the cosmos, but
constellations are the imaginary lines we draw between
them, the readings we give the sky, the stories we tell.

REBECCA SOLNIT

*S*tellar constellations prove glorious examples of pareidolia, the perception of meaningful images in random aggregations. These recognitions often take human forms. We see the man in the moon, eyes in the exteriors of houses, celebrities in clouds.

Pareidolia is more than whimsy. It is wired in our brains. The neurons of the fusiform gyrus have evolved to recognize facial features. We must discern faces to survive. If you can recognize a friend's face over an enemy's, for example, or infer emotions behind facial expressions, then you are more likely to form valuable social bonds. Likewise, a hunter prone to perceiving animal faces in the near distance is on average more successful, even if his visions sometimes amount to nothing more than pareidolia.

As a survival skill, pareidolia is comforting: a translation of the strange into the familiar. But while the familiar is useful, it is also monotonous. Wherever you look, you see what you expect. If you expect human forms, especially faces, you see your kind everywhere. The world becomes a mirror.

What is creativity but the ability to shatter the glass, to discover in the scatters not time-worn forms but "figures in quick movement, and strange expressions of faces, and outlandish costumes, and an infinite number of things"? These are Da Vinci's words; they describe the origin of his art: disorienting pareidolia, the gift for sensing in the strange the even stranger.

To refresh your connection to your world, project, like Da Vinci, your own unsettling figures. Do so first among the strewn stars. Your goal: constellate without recourse to faces, bodies, known technologies.

Locate outlandish arrays. Maybe something trapped between a torus and a balbis. Or perhaps an undiscovered bacteria. Or why not some eldritch shape from your most private mind?

You can find all the forms you fling, since immense assemblages eventually will cohere, or appear to cohere, into what we project.

Once you have made your uncanny constellation, go to your notebook. Title a blank page "Astral Pareidolia." Now draw your image and describe how it has altered your relationship to the stars. Set aside three more pages. Once a week for the next three weeks, repeat this exercise.

If you enjoy this activity, give it its own notebook. It will prove a survival guide to your inner wilderness.

11.

Construct a Curvilinear Terrarium

*N*eurologists at the Zanvyl Krieger Mind/Brain Institute have shown that rounded forms "produce stronger responses and increased activity in the brain," probably because "shallow convex surface curvature" typifies living organisms, such as eyes, muscles, and brains themselves.

What curvilinear shapes do you love? Conchs? Acorns? Eggshells? Stones from the river?

Whatever they are, arrange them in a goldfish bowl, among jagged pebbles and moss and a plant (like boxwood or Joseph's coat), and look at them every morning for a minute or two.

These orbs mirror back your own mind's roundness and remind you—in a world all-too-often lacerated by points—of the virtues of curves, whorls, vortices, spirals, eddies, circles, and spheres.

12.

Contrive a Shrine
for Colors

*C*olors mirror moods, and they often reflect feelings we weren't quite aware we were harboring. They are also mood makers, inspiring fresh emotions. Call them archives as well, since they appear to hold within them the memories they evoke.

To say you have a favorite color is really to say, "I am in a certain mood right now." If you were to contemplate your color's complexity, you would experience your mood more intensely and expansively. It would increase and radiate.

My mood right now is blue. I think of the ocean and melancholia, but that is just the beginning. A blue sky expresses the very heavens, while a blue movie is porn. "Once in a blue moon" means rare. Blue is the most infrequent color in nature, but the tusks of the wooly mammoth were blueish ivory. Cats with blue eyes are prone to deafness. The owl is the only bird that can see blue.

Corpses, because of cyanosis, are blue, and Mayans painted blue the chests of their sacrificial victims, whose hearts they carved out. Kandinsky said, "The deeper blue becomes, the more urgently it summons man toward the infinite." Katherine Mansfield exclaimed, "Very beautiful, O God! is a blue tea-pot with two white cups attending."

The male satin bowerbird gathers blue objects to create his love shack. Hydrangea petals, grape hyacinth, blue jay feathers, indigo bunting, bits of blue plastic bags, blue paper, blue butterfly wings. He also paints his bower with bluish fruit juices: blueberry, blackberry, grape. For a brush, he uses a twig with frayed ends. Once his trysting pad is done, he does a mating dance in front of it.

What is your color right now, your mood? Write the color at the top of a page. Free associate, attaching the hue to as many facts and fantasies as you can, as well as to memories, poems, novels, films, songs.

Now create a shrine to the color's splendors. It can be a shoebox turned on its side, or an empty bookshelf, or just a spot on your nightstand. Whatever the space, fill it with mementos. For blue, I would array the shells of robin eggs, or bottle caps (Labatt Blue, Blue Moon), or blue "Admit One" tickets, or a blue ribbon, or the wing of an eastern tailed-blue.

When your mood changes, return your tokens to the world, and make an altar for your new spirits.

13.

Quest for Your Daemon

*Like the ostrich, I cannot fly, yet I have wings that give
me the feeling of flight.*

SAMUEL TAYLOR COLERIDGE

In "The Raven," Poe's speaker wonders if the spooky bird is a demon, not only in the Christian sense of evil spirit but also in the Socratic one: daemon as deep self.

Philip Pullman dramatizes this latter notion. Each of his characters in *His Dark Materials* is accompanied by an animal who expresses the person's essence. Pullman has admitted that his own daemon is the raven, because it "belongs to that family of birds that steal things." He applauds this "enterprising way of dealing with the world."

Choose your own feathery daemon.

Out of the thousands of kinds of birds, which one speaks to you? Where to begin your search?

Think of the birds that enchanted your childhood, like those of nursery rhymes, the four-and-twenty blackbirds, the fine cuckoo who tells no lies, Goosey Gander, Robin Redbreast. Or what about the real robin, whose worm hunting first revealed that life lives on killing? Or the mother mockingbird, who fights off even hawks to protect her eggs?

Maybe you connect with a bird in a poem. Obviously, there is the nightingale of Keats, Dickinson's hummingbird, Gerard Manley Hopkins's windhover. But also Tyree Daye's "blackbirds with nowhere to go" but who "keep leaving"; and Dorianne Laux's "red-breasted" bird whose "click, swoosh, thump" is the sound of her trying to break in the window; and Louise Bogan's pheasants milling about the marble statue of a girl, "closed up in their arrowy wings / Dragging their sharp tails." Note, too, the plover of Bashō, who in "a night of darkness," having "lost its nest," cries out; or his hawk, whose darkening eyes lose the quail.

Maybe outlandish birds attract you, ones you've seen in documentaries: the helmeted hornbill or the marabou stork. Or perhaps you enjoy famous symbols: peacocks, owls, doves, condors.

Regardless of where you search, make sure the daemon bird calls forth what you find most interesting about yourself: your wit, say, or compassion or strength or wackiness or verbosity or musicality or mischievousness.

Once you have lighted on your bird, memorize a passage of poetry describing it; if you can't find your bird in verse, write your own lines. Display a painting, sketch, or photograph of your bird. Draw it yourself.

In being closer to this bird, you are nearer to yourself. And what is this intimacy but an understanding of how you will stand against gravity?

14.

Quiver a Witch Stick

*D*owsers—or diviners, or doodlebuggers, or water witches—cradle in their hands the forks of their Y-shaped rod. They walk over stretches of land, and when they sense a quiver in their implement, and it dips, they cry, "Dig here!" Again, so they hope, they have detected underground water, or perhaps oil, ores, corpses, even gems.

Dowsers began plying their craft in the sixteenth century, and it has flourished ever since, even though Martin Luther in 1518 deemed the divining rod a tool of Satanic magic. The theory is that certain people enjoy acute sensitivity to the earth's magnetic field, and so they can detect spots where groundwater or buried metal alters the current. The forked rod—usually a twig or a small branch of wood but sometimes metal—indicates the subtle disturbance.

Scientists now believe that the stick's tilt results from an ideomotor response, or an unconscious bodily twitch, and that the diviner's so-called successes are simply random.

But doodlebugging persists. Marines during the Vietnam War divined for subterranean weapons, and in 1986 Norwegian soldiers did the same to find victims of an avalanche. The American Society of Dowsers boasts 2,000 active members.

There are other reasons to dowse than seeking things underground, however. Do some divining yourself to see what I mean.

In a forest or park, or on a tree-lined street, harvest a fallen or low-hanging branch, thin and limber, and snap here and there to approximate a "Y." Turn your hands skyward; let each hold lightly the end of a prong. Point the tail forward.

Doesn't this supple wishbone feel good in your hands?

Now walk slowly over an area of your choice; bare earth or pavement, doesn't matter.

Even if there's no magic, keep your eyes on the ground and be alert to the rod's least tremor. Passing thus, you reimagine your relation to the earth.

You wonder: Is there an occult connection between me and the invisible? Magnetic forces course within me, and within the soil, so maybe I and this terrain are patterns of the same ubiquitous energy. Perhaps I am not discrete, but distributed through the universe, never alone.

Now ease away from cosmic contemplation, and just study the ground. Attend to the anthill, out of which crawls an orange ant; the color of the sunny grass, emerald crossed with silver; the paper clip rusting beside the ground-in gum.

The witch stick is a movie camera, encouraging close-ups and wide shots. It is also a pleasure meter, now registering the abundance of the cosmos, now the ground's exquisite textures.

15.

Drink Air

Everybody who's anybody longs to be a tree.

RITA DOVE

*P*lants only use about 10 percent of the water they draw up through their roots. The remainder evaporates through petals, stems, and leaves. The name for this conversion of water into nutrition, and then air, is transpiration.

For poet Arthur Sze, transpiration symbolizes our ability to attune to the universe. Just as transpiration pulls subterranean liquid up through the plant's stalk and sends it into the atmosphere, so we can, like "the edges of leaves," express our deepest interiors to the universe.

But raw expression isn't the only way to channel transpiration. You can also sip the spirit.

On a sunny day, choose a tree. It should not have been sprayed with pesticide.

Cover the tip of a leafy branch with a medium-sized plastic bag, clear. Tie the opening tightly around the branch.

The bag must sag below the branch.

After an hour, droplets appear, and flow to the lowest point.

Three hours later, significant water has collected.

Remove the bag.

Pour the water into a glass.

Drink the water.

16.

Novelize a Thrift Store

*I*n our mass-produced world, everything feels the same. According to psychologist Jennifer Baumgartner, this is why we love the thrift store, where there is only *one* of this thing. I can cherish its rareness as I would a living creature, unprecedented and unrepeatable.

Other attractions of the thrift shop are the pleasures of hunting for nothing in particular and finding something remarkable; the satisfying weights (real wood, actual metal) and textures (the thick stitching, the sturdy fabric) of vintage goods; and the nostalgia of roaming among bygone styles.

But isn't the greatest draw of thrifting the pleasure of speculating about the history of the merchandise? Who spent his evenings, martini in hand, relaxing in this recliner? What occasions inspired someone to sport this faux mink coat? Who bought this paperback biography of Lynda Carter, new?

Enter a thrift store in search of clues to the lives behind the items. Discreetly search the pockets of men's suits, the interiors of purses and luggage, the drawers of desks, the crevices of couches. Flip through the pages of books.

You might find a dollar or two, but that's not what you're after; you want remnants. Dry cleaning tickets, concert tickets, tickets for delis, grocery receipts, receipts from mechanics, receipts from psychiatrists and liquor stores, Post-it Notes with phone numbers or passwords, paper scraps penned with one word you can't make out, golf tees, cough drops, small Phillips head screws, chewed gum wrapped in cocktail napkins, breath mints, business cards, candy-bar wrappers, keys, used Band-Aids, guitar picks, buttons.

Take your object home.

Imagine its owner.

Handwrite a three-sentence biography of this person.

Store the keepsake in a box.

Stuff the bio in a suit pocket at the thrift store.

17.

Transform Trash into Art

Perfection is less interesting. For instance, a page
with a poem on it is less attractive than a page with a
poem on it and some tea stains. Because the tea stains
add a bit of history.

ANNE CARSON

*I*n thrift shopping you don't know the past owner of your purchase. When you buy at a garage sale, the opposite is true. And not only do you meet the owner; you often have a conversation about what you are buying.

The contact between the seller and buyer is a primary pleasure of the garage sale. The seller enjoys telling the buyer the history of the item and relishes the transfer to someone who appreciates its meaning. In turn, the buyer happily obtains a special object, and he prizes his role as a protector.

Of course, not all garage sale merchandise carries positive meanings. In some cases, the seller wants to get rid of a painful article, like a wedding dress from a broken marriage; in other instances, she simply wants to purge clutter.

On a Saturday morning, during the fall, go to a garage sale (or yard or stoop sale) and engage the seller in conversations about items that interest you. Purchase the one—if affordable—whose story you find the most charming.

Now that you own the object—a Bugs Bunny glass, dingy Barbie, commemorative "Who Shot J.R.?" beer can, thimble, owl clock with moving eyes, *Life* magazine from '63, orange macramé pot holder, self-hypnosis manual, shuttlecock—what will you do with it?

Turn it into a work of art that reflects its story. For instance, if the owner acquired the self-hypnosis manual to stop smoking, maybe carve a rectangular recess into its pages and make the front cover into a lid, and you have a faux cigarette box.

Once finished, display the work in your dwelling and tell your friends its story. If they are interested, offer to sell it to them.

18.

Haunt Your Haunts

*The more you love a memory, the stronger and
stranger it is.*

VLADIMIR NABOKOV

*O*ne night, when he was a boy, William Wordsworth stole a boat. As he plunged the oars, he saw a mountain, ominous and black, rise in the horizon, and higher rise, until it blocked the stars. It appeared to leap onto the lake and harry him across the water. After, he was not the same; usurping his habitual thoughts were "huge and mighty Forms that do not live / Like living men."

The adult Wordsworth prizes this moment, its intermingling of terror and ecstasy. Such mysterious "spots of time" mark when we are most alive, and they make us who we fundamentally are.

How to activate these memories?

Sometimes the most random event—the offhand tasting of a madeleine crumbled in tea—will evoke a whole childhood, as it did for Marcel Proust. But a more predictable technique for conjuring our essential memories is to visit their places of origin.

We all have nostalgic haunts: that hill where you had your first kiss, or the skate park still decorated with your graffiti, or the library where you first read your favorite YA novel.

Then there are the more secret locales, where things happened you didn't tell your parents about: the bleachers where you failed at sex and hurled from Smirnoff, the riverbank where you backed down from a fight.

But what about the places where the really weird shit went down, things you've never told *anybody* about? These are the sources of your most potent memories—startling, enigmatic, formative.

The woods where you found those decayed *Hustlers* while you were playing Capture the Flag. The backyard where you happened upon your math teacher sunbathing topless when you were taking the shortcut home from school. Your dad's toolshed, where you found that long blonde hair.

When you reach these strange places, stand there for five minutes with your eyes closed, imagining the memory as clearly as you can. Then take out your notebook and describe the scene. Don't worry about grammar or syntax. Focus more on concrete details— the stark "is-ness" of the event. And don't try too hard to figure out what the memory means. It probably means nothing, other than the world is strange, and most vital when most strange. Channeling this inscrutable energy, you feel enlivened yourself, and, if you are sad, renovated.

19.

Rearrange Your Childhood Bedroom

*I*magine: a seemingly benevolent demon has just told you that you can switch three objects in your childhood bedroom for any other three objects that you desire, and that you can rearrange the newly equipped room any way you would like. Now draw a floor plan of this room and then answer the question: If I had grown up in this room, how would my life have turned out differently?

20.

Celebrate the
Uninteresting Stuff

*I*n October of 1974, Georges Perec spent three straight days in Paris's Place Saint-Sulpice. His purpose was not to pay attention to the grand architecture but rather the small stuff, "that which is generally not taken note of, that which is not noticed, that which has no importance: what happens when nothing happens other than the weather, people, cars, and clouds."

Perec's focus on the ordinary did for him what sitting a long time in one place, out-of-doors, in your town, can do for you: invited things to shine forth as things that are simply *things*, not "examples of," "segues to," "substitutes for," "distractions from," only as this, here, now.

For one day, stage your own Perecian sit-down. Situate yourself at a seemingly trivial place and record all the details you can. At the end of the day, list in your notebook at least five things you noticed that you had not noticed before. How has this new awareness altered your relationship to the locale?

21.

Get a Zero

A student in a class on Zen Buddhism turned in a research paper composed of ten blank sheets. He believed his professor would conclude that he understood the essence of Zen—all form is emptiness—and give him an A.

The professor gave the student a zero. When the student challenged the grade, the professor said, "To the true student of Zen, nothingness is bliss."

The professor was invoking Śūnyatā, voidness: the things of the world possess no intrinsic meaning but are ephemeral renderings of the nonbeing from which they arise and to which they will return. There is nothing to hold on to. When we try to pin permanent meaning on an object, we doom ourselves to sorrow, since the thing will not stay still.

To feel ease, even happiness, is to embrace the transience, knowing that the meanings we impose onto the world—and we can't *not* impose meaning—are provisional, valuable as long as they are useful, to be revised or replaced when not.

Once a day for a week, place a valuable object in front of you.

Could be a piece of jewelry, an heirloom, a fifty-dollar bill, a diploma, a trophy, a favorite book, a photo of a loved one. Anything.

Stare at the object, and imagine that it is a hologram, and picture yourself floating within the colored air of the phantasm, and then becoming an apparition yourself. Now fancy that your ghostly self is looking at your solid self. Hold this bizarre scene in your head as long as you can, before your imagination tires, and the world once more solidifies and appears stable.

This exercise will save you from being overly attached to things, too dependent upon them for your happiness. It will also relax your possessiveness. You will become more likely to let things be, instead of saying to them, *mine*.

22.

Alienate Yourself from Yourself

A witch appears to you in a forest, and she says, "Deep down, at one point in your life, you have desired to become something not human, even if for an instant. An animal, perhaps, or a color, or an element; maybe a cloud or stone. Because I am bored, I will grant you the ability to become this thing, for no more than an hour, while still retaining your own identity. What would you choose to be?"

Answer her question in your notebook, and then write a first-person paragraph from your thing's point of view. At the end of the paragraph, come back to yourself and ask: Am I different now, having been something else, and, if so, how has my heart stretched?

23.

Memorize a Poem
Peripatetically

*W*ere you forced to memorize a poem in grade school? These days, probably not. Why bother to memorize verse when your smartphone puts you a tap or two away from almost every poem ever published? The utility of remembering a poem very real in the old days, when access to books was limited—has gone the way of the daguerreotype.

But uselessness is exactly the reason to imprint a poem in your mind. That you don't need the knowledge to thrive in the world invites verse memorization into the category of graceful superfluity, like dancing, tennis, or lepidoptery.

But maybe memorizing a poem is more than passing time pleasantly. Brad Leithauser suggests that taking a poem to heart doesn't so much ease time as deepen it: "You take the poem inside you, into your brain chemistry if not your blood, and you know it at a deeper, bodily level than if you simply read it off a screen." The rhythms of the lines and those of your heart echo one another. You become a breathing poem.

Even without this mingling of blood and ballad, the memorizing would still prove exhilarating. It intensifies our passages through this earth. Recite Gwendolyn Brooks's "We Real Cool" while you walk, and you step more deftly, and Brooks's "lurk" and "strike" make the world risky.

Memorize a short poem, but do it while walking. The verse rhythms will inform your very sinews, and your stride will shape the song. And just as your motion feels more agile, so your perception will expand, since in the poem's lens, your path opens into a plenitude.

24.

Comb Plato's Beard

*R*iddler: I have billions of eyes, yet I live in darkness. I have millions of ears, yet only four lobes. I have no muscle, yet I rule two hemispheres. What am I?

Batman. The human brain.

If you lived in ancient Greece, a riddle wasn't an equation; it was a revelation. Plato, for instance, relied on enigmatic allegories to hint at the mystery of being—and nothingness. What Willard Van Orman Quine called the riddle of Plato's beard refers to the revered philosopher's idea that "Nonbeing must in some sense be, otherwise what is it that there is not?" This tangled doctrine dulls Occam's razor.

Plato lived in a time of oracles, when priestesses inhaled heady fumes and babbled of futures. This influenced his mingling of inscrutability and truth. Medieval Europeans likewise imagined riddles as God-speak. The universe is the Deity's arcane book, and each creature a darkish rendering of his light.

The playful koans of Zen in this context converse with somber theology. The Zen riddles—"What is the color of wind?"—short-circuit reason and inspire extraordinary intuitions.

No wonder Emily Dickinson, whose poems read like koans ("A Bomb upon the Ceiling / is an improving thing"), believed "The Riddle we can guess / We speedily despise—."

Compose your own riddle, but make sure it is not easily solved. View it less as a question to be answered and more as an inspiration to think.

Send this riddle to three friends, explaining its purpose. Ask each to reply with their own solution.

What do these answers tell you that you didn't know before?

25.

Irritate a Narcissist

Compose a riddle with no solution on a Post-it Note. Secretly paste the note to a mirror in a public bathroom.

Here are some examples of open-ended puzzlers.

> What do you get when you cross a manatee and a dream?
>
> Two plus tractor equals (a) hog (b) place where she never (c) weather drip.
>
> What's egg and confused and wobbly top-side?

Invent other such riddles, the more enigmatic the better, and write them on other Post-it Notes. Whenever you find yourself in a public bathroom, paste a riddle.

Do this at least seven times.

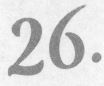

26.

Listen to the Glass Wizard

*Y*ou are a mirror in an airport bathroom. A wizard made of crystal tells you that you can change into a lens in the glasses of the next bespectacled person who gazes into you, or remain what you are. What would you do?

27.

Snort a Quarto

Second-hand books are wild books.

VIRGINIA WOOLF

The paper in books is composed of cellulose and lignin. As these decay over time, chemical compounds—such as ethyl benzene, toluene, and furfural—dissolve and emanate an odor, a "combination," according to a team of chemists, "of grassy notes with a tang of acids and a hint of vanilla over an underlying mustiness."

This is why old books smell like they smell, and the smell is thrilling.

Visit a used bookstore. Mosey on over to your favorite section. Browse. Do you see your favorite book from childhood? A more recent love? Maybe a title you've been meaning to read?

Whichever book speaks to you most, pull it from the shelf, hold it in both hands, look at it. You are going to open this book and *sniff* it.

When you do, strong memories will arise—the texture of the cover of your eighth-grade science book, maybe, or the dim green room where your grandmother kept her books, mostly historical fiction, or the first time you read this particular title (you had just come out of a fever).

Your whiff might feel like a miracle: an inanimate object is *alive* in your hands. Kindles and Nooks and iPads are fine for reading, but these slabs of metal and plastic don't decay into odors as an actual creature does.

What else might you feel when you put your nose in the book? Hard to say, there are so many possibilities, but whatever happens, it will almost certainly be good, since books are intelligence, empathy, beauty, patience, writing in margins, cool bookmarks, colorful spines, flipping to your favorite page, stacking, shelving, going somewhere else that's better than where you are.

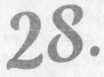

28.

Fabricate a Story That Has Never Existed Before

If there's a book that you want to read, but it hasn't been written yet, then you must write it.

TONI MORRISON

*T*he world-weary narrator of Ecclesiastes observed, "There is nothing new under the sun." He was expressing that depressive feeling that usually comes, oddly enough, when the seasons change: everything that's going to happen has already happened, many times, and you're doomed to experience the same damn thing over and over and over. Been there, done that. Seen one, seen 'em all.

When you're in this mood, and you crave newness, you've got to draw on the perennial source of novelty: randomness. As Salmon Rushdie observes, "Mélange, hotchpotch, a bit of this and a bit of that is how newness enters the world." Throw this and that together, stir, and toss more stuff in, stir some more, and there: you've got something that didn't exist before. It might not be that good, but at least it's different, and sometimes that's enough.

Here is one of millions of ways to make something new.

At the top of a piece of blank paper, write the first sentence of a short story that does not exist, as far as you know, but that you would like to read.

Fold the paper up and slip it in your pocket and go to a library. Take a pencil.

Visit your favorite section. Shut your eyes, pull out the first book you touch.

Open your eyes, open to a random page. What is the first sentence? Write it under the sentence you brought into the library.

Return the book. Now turn around to the row of shelves behind you. Once more, close your eyes, choose a book, open to a page. Copy its last sentence under the one from the last book.

You have three sentences.

This is the first paragraph of a two-page story you will now write by hand.

Under the sun, it will be new.

29.

Review Books
That Do Not Exist

*P*olish science fiction writer Stanislaw Lem has composed three collections of reviews of books that don't exist. *A Perfect Vacuum*, for example, contains notices of fifteen fictional books, including *U-Write-It*, a "literary erector set" made up of blank pages and fragments from great novels; *Les Robinsonades,* about a castaway who fills his time trying, and failing, to create a world in his imagination; and *Rien du tout, ou la consequence*, in which all sentences are negations ("The train did not arrive. He did not come.")

If a common theme runs through the fake books, it is, appropriately, world-building, either by humans or computers. But play seems to be the point: Lem appears to relish the comic absurdity of his titles, as well as to enjoy parodying the pretentious erudition of reviewers.

Writing can sometimes be a game for the sake of a game, which is of course the best kind of game, since winning and losing aren't the point, only the playing is, the verve and brio of it.

To channel Lem's gusto, create three (or more) fake titles of your own and then write one-sentence reviews in voices other than your own. For instance:

Bunting. Yes! by Dice Pungle.

If Emily Post and Albert Camus had a child, it would be Pungle, whose debut novel is a deadpan celebration of paper at its most crinkled.

Negative Moon Nine by Symonds McClellan.

Obelisks, gouache, a comedian, interstellar dread, Endymion: McClellan has done it again, a tour de force of galactic mayhem, but this time, perhaps because of his well-known personal tragedy, with heart.

Collywobbles Wax: A Scarlett O'Tarot Mystery by Renata Stanhope.

Our favorite young sleuth is on the case once more, this time infiltrating a secret network of wax museums, only to find that sometimes statues are more silent than they seem.

30.

Imagine Your Life as a Peculiar Novel Written by a Lazy God

A bookish angel visits you in a dream. She tells you that you aren't an actual person but a character in a novel currently being written by an obscure demigod. This god is tired of the story and plans to give up on it. The only way you can continue to exist is if you get him interested in your life again. You can achieve this by doing something that you've never done before and that will almost certainly yield strangely compelling results.

You wake up and take the angel seriously enough to describe, in writing, what this action would be, and what would likely follow.

Will you do this thing? Why or why not?

31.

Crank Some Microfilm

Perhaps our eyes are merely a blank film which is taken from us after our deaths to be developed elsewhere and screened as our life story in some infernal cinema or dispatched as microfilm into the sidereal void.

JEAN BAUDRILLARD

*I*n 1839, daguerreotypist John Benjamin Dancer of Manchester learned to shrink photographs to microscopic scales. By the 1850s, he was reducing cityscapes to 1 mm and mounting the images on microscope slides. Victorians gazing through the lenses lost themselves in endless alleyways.

Soon Parisian inventor René Dagron created jewelry whose gemstones were miniature lenses opening onto diminutive pictures, sometimes of huge crowds of people. During the Siege of Paris (1870–71), Dagron produced Lilliputian-sized military documents for pigeons to fly across enemy lines. Recipients affixed the images to a glass frame and, with a magic lantern, projected them onto a wall.

These are early applications of microfilm. The medium has continued to figure in warfare. During the Cold War, for instance, the Soviet Union hid a microfilmed message to one of its spies in a hollow nickel. But microfilm's main purpose has been archival. Imagine the delight of librarians when they learned they could reduce up to 2,500 documents to 100 feet of film wrapped elegantly around a 16 mm spool. Now the contents of decaying documents could be preserved, and hundreds of square feet freed.

Even though digitization has replaced microfilm as the primary mode of data preservation, most libraries still house the medium as the sole preserver of many old newspapers.

Visit your local library and ask to view a microfilm version of a newspaper—any paper will do, as long as it's available in this medium. Announce a particular day you wish to research. Could be your birthday, the birthday of a loved one, a day of historical significance, or just some random day.

The librarian will likely lead you into a dark, out-of-the-way room. There you behold what looks like an old TV, whose bluish-green screen is 12.5 inches across, 17 high. Sit before the screen, wait for the librarian to return with your film. You sniff a hint of vinegar. The last researcher must have perused acetate microfilm, versus the newer polyester stock, mostly odorless. The librarian returns, and they hand you a tan cardboard box the size of a large bar of soap. They remove a spool of film. Polyester. Regardless of who does the loading, enjoy the "click" of the spool fitting onto the feeder at the left, and then the sliding of the stock under the glass, and the threading of the film into the take-up reel on the right. The librarian leaves. Crank the take-up reel, and relish the soft hum, and watch the images race across the screen. You reach your chosen day.

Notice what is lacking in digital transcriptions: *context*. News stories surround other news stories. Their size and position suggest their relative importance. But it's not all journalism. Check out the paper's fonts and layout, as well its advertisements and perhaps its classifieds scattered over the page. Then there are the accidental effects of the actual film; maybe the image is a little blurry here, dark there.

What you are witnessing is how events interacted on a given day from the past, as well as the circumstances at play when the periodical was actually photographed.

Browse through the pages of the day you have chosen until you find a story that captures you. Read the story, study its surroundings on the page.

In a notebook, write down three ways this revelation of the past speaks to you. Then answer these questions: Do I have a new sense of my history, however small and subtle? What is it?

After you've answered, keep browsing until the soft light makes you dreamy and hungry for a meal.

32.

Welcome the Earworm

*Ε*arworm: that song that repeats in your head, all day, and you can't shut it down, and you don't even really like it.

Certain songs are more likely to become earworms. Faster songs, for instance, with beats that are easy to dance to. Also songs that feature simple structures and strong rhythms, usually with a clear rise and fall, like a nursery rhyme. But the song can't be too predictable; the pattern must break unexpectedly, cleverly.

According to a survey, the most common earworms among recent songs include Maroon 5's "Moves Like Jagger," Katy Perry's "California Gurls," and three by Lady Gaga: "Bad Romance," "Alejandro," and "Poker Face." Older sticky songs are "Don't Stop Believin'" and "Bohemian Rhapsody."

These are good songs. But that doesn't mean we want them in our heads all day. Too much repetition makes anything irritating, and what about the other thoughts and memories, possibly enlightening, this song is crowding out? And what if the song isn't that great, but top forty schlock left over from high school?

What if the song takes over your mind? In Arthur C. Clarke's story "The Ultimate Melody," a scientist creates a pop tune that corresponds perfectly to the rhythms of his brain; the music bewitches him into catatonia. Henry Kuttner in "Nothing but Gingerbread Left" describes a similar song—but the results are happier. The tune is so catchy, it infiltrates Hitler's mind and distracts him to the point that he can't deliver an important speech.

On the internet you can find advice for how to avoid earworms. Don't listen to music in the first place. Chew gum. Sing your own songs. Talk to a friend. Relax, and your mind will move on to something else.

I say, welcome earworms. When one comes, and it will, write out the lyrics to the tune. Pretend like the song is an experimental work of your favorite author, perhaps a campy satire, but maybe a straight-up expression of strong emotion. At the bottom of the page, pen the name of the author. Pretend that this person created these lines.

For instance, I get a Toto earworm: "Africa." I sign my transcription of their lyrics "Frank O'Hara," my favorite twentieth-century poet.

Whatever way you imagine the intention, the annoying song is now different, since it is by an esteemed writer; the writer is now different, since he has written a too-addictive song; and a new relationship has entered the world: the bizarre marriage of a song you've had too much of and a writer of whom you can't get enough.

Conceive a Curse Word

*It's how a person would talk when a famous poet died
and everyone was oh he was so beautiful with his
white hair walking through Harvard Yard. It's a class
thing and a young poet thinking fuck him, fuck the
poetry world's reverence for wasps and their well
preserved and honored beauty.*

EILEEN MYLES

*C*ursing can save you.

A recent study asked participants to immerse their hands in ice water; those who swore during the ordeal endured the pain longest. Cursing assuages emotional discomfort. When we are frustrated by a situation we can't control—such as being stranded in an airport—spewing expletives relieves our stress. Profanity also fosters community; you curse with your closest friends, and swearing with acquaintances forms new bonds. Cursing marks intelligence; potty mouths tend to be more verbally adroit, better educated. Dirty talk is, moreover, the glee of taboo-breaking.

And then there is obscenity's poetry. Who wouldn't delight in these old sex profanities? Rantallion (scrotum longer than penis), clatterdevengance (penis), grope for the trout in a peculiar river (cheating sex), ringerangeroo (vagina), gamahuche (oral sex), give the green grown to (sex on the grass), pogue the hone (sex), chapel of ease (vagina).

Let swearing's lyricism, not to mention its therapeutic virtues, inspire you to conceive your own curses.

Beginners can simply take existing swears and G-rate them, in the tradition of "mother-loving mother-lover." Here are some examples: "cork maker," "frocking dressmaker," "grog dram."

More ambitious types might get historical, tweaking old-fashioned profanity to suit their fancy. You can morph "dad-sizzle" ("goddamn") into "dim bittle," or "cacafuego" ("fire-shitter") into "facacargo."

Another higher order curse creation model: borrow a name. Appellations already made foul include "Judas Priest" and "William Shatner." When my dad was a kid, he and his friends made the name of the meanest man in town into a curse: "Con Hester!" You might search your memory and do the same.

But why not aspire to the pinnacle and concoct a curse sui generis? Write down the name of a person you really f-ing hate. Now write a sound that captures the person's essence. For instance, if you were to detest "Doug from two doors down," you might write "dod-cad!" Is the sound fun to say? Then you have your own curse.

When stressed, invoke your vulgarity.

34.

Hatch an Aphorism

There's a basic humility to the aphorist who takes as a
given the impossibility of knowing more than a grain
of sand here, a woodpecker's knock there. Or is it a
basic hubris—as though the world and human nature
were knowable from the smallest detail? But isn't that
precisely the double-edged quality of lyric poetry, its
humble arrogance in its small assertions of truth?

SHARON DOLIN

*H*ippocrates (c. 460–370 BCE) introduced the aphorism—from the
Greek for "definition"—in a work on medicine. His numbered prop-
ositions are pithy and clever, beginning with the first and most
famous one: "Life is short, art is long."

The aphorism evolved into a literary form: the concise, memorable, frequently witty expression of traditional wisdom. The best
aphorisms require interpretation. They are dense and dazzling,
like poems. Take Emerson's "To be great is to be misunderstood";
or Dickinson's "Forever—is composed of Nows"; or James Bald-
win's "Anyone who has ever struggled with poverty knows how

extremely expensive it is to be poor"; or Valeria Luiselli's "Words arranged in the right order produce an afterglow."

Some writers push the wit of the aphorism to such an extreme that the aphorism reverses itself and becomes an anti-aphorism: an undercutting of truisms. The master of this technique is Oscar Wilde.

> *I can resist everything except temptation.*

> *Always forgive your enemies; nothing annoys them so much.*

> *To love oneself is the beginning of a lifelong romance.*

In each case, Wilde sets us up to expect a clichéd moral—we should not give into temptation, we should forgive our enemies, we should not be egocentric—but then counters that very maxim: we are unable to resist temptation, we should harass our enemies, we should love ourselves forever. The effect is double vision, a perception of a principle and its contrary at the same time. The irony is of course unsettling, but it also invites us to coordinate oppositions.

More recent comedians have followed Wilde's lead.

> *Looking fifty is great—if you're sixty.* —JOAN RIVERS

> *I think God made babies cute, so we don't eat them.*
> —ROBIN WILLIAMS

> *Accept who you are. Unless you are a serial killer.*
> —ELLEN DEGENERES

> *A man is only as faithful as his options.* —CHRIS ROCK

Create your own paradoxical witticism. Start out with a terse statement of conventional wisdom and then comically challenge it. Here are some examples I've come up with.

Live this day as if it's your last, and you will run around screaming, "I'm going to fucking die!"

Never go to bed angry; drunk is much better.

Failure isn't final; it's also at the beginning and in the middle.

The purpose of this exercise is twofold: it will push you to think outside of habitual parameters and it will cultivate the oddness of irony: "is" superimposed on "is not."

35.

Conjure Your Own Medieval Monster

A monster is a person who has stopped pretending.

COLSON WHITEHEAD

A man's head, body of a lion, a scorpion's tail: this is a manticore.

A monoceros has a horse body, boar tail, elephant feet, head of a stag, one black horn.

A person with no head is a Blemmyes. He has a face, however, on his chest.

Cynocephali: dog-headed people.

These medieval monsters explode categories. A man is a lion is a scorpion.

Monsters unsettle us because they violate the basis of all logic: something can't be A and not-A at the same time. Without this distinction, all is chaos.

But chaos can liberate us from life's stifling demarcations.

Make your own monster. Notice four things close to you this minute. Quickly sketch each one separately and then draw them mashed, somehow, together. Give the creature a name.

When you are embarrassed, remember that your monster, an unspeakable hodgepodge, far transcends the shame of a single ego. You will feel better.

36.

Chinwag with Your Evil Twin

*T*here is only a one in one trillion chance that someone in the world looks exactly like you. Because of the small number of facial characteristics, however, the odds of near resemblance are good. Over half the population has brown eyes, for instance; one fourth, fleshy noses; ten percent, round faces.

Percy Bysshe Shelley claimed he saw a "figure of himself" out on his terrace, and it said to him, "'How long do you mean to be content?'" The poet died soon after.

Our narcissism is aroused when friends tell us we resemble celebrities. But that is rare. More likely someone in the Walmart looks like you. You are just a face in the crowd.

This is why we love the idea of having an alter ego, an evil twin, who doesn't reinforce our ordinariness but makes us *conflicted*, *tortured*, and therefore dramatic, interesting.

If your evil twin is the opposite of you, then what would they be like? Describe your twin in a brief paragraph.

Now imagine running into your double while you are out walking, at twilight. You walk together for a time. What three questions would you ask? What answers do you think you would receive?

Now what questions would they ask you, and how would you respond?

At the end of the conversation, do you admire your twin more or less than you thought? Do you believe your twin thinks positively of you or negatively?

Once you've answered these questions, you'll have a deeper understanding of what you fear and what you love.

37.

Dress Your Döppelganger

Aside from what your evil twin wears on the day you meet, what are their other favorite outfits? Describe three of them. What does their villain couture say about your clothing?

38.

Journey to the Uncanny Valley

Where grace is concerned, it is impossible for man to come anywhere near a puppet.

HEINRICH VON KLEIST

*M*asahiro Mori studies automaton spookiness. When a robot approaches a humanlike appearance, observers respond positively. But if the robot becomes barely distinguishable from a human, observers are revulsed. A robot that resembles a human exactly, however, turns the response favorable again, since humans feel they can relate to the android as they relate to each other.

Mori's "uncanny valley"—the rise, dip, and re-rise of positive response toward the automaton—suggests that androids inseparable from us are comforting, since they reinforce our traditional notions of the "human."

For an entire day, imagine that everyone around you is a robot indistinguishable from a human. How does this perception change your feelings about them? The next day, imagine that everyone sees *you* as a robot. Does their behavior toward you seem different?

Reflect on these two days. Make two columns on a page, side by side. In the left column, list five adjectives that describe how you felt when you pictured yourself surrounded by automatons. In the right, list five descriptors of what you think others would feel about you if they thought you were an artificial human.

Are the lists identical? If so, decide if the similarity is a result of empathy (your ability to feel your way inside the heads of others) or if the parallels result from egotism (your assumption that others simply perceive the world like you do).

If there are discrepancies in the list, does this mean that you believe that others are wired differently than you? If so, does the disparity signal your antagonism toward them, or your effort to respect their otherness?

Once you have completed this exercise, you have compared human and robot behavior, imagined how you and others view the same phenomenon, and contemplated your attitude toward the feelings of others.

You have in essence sketched what you see as your "humanity."

Are you proud of it?

39.

Consider a Victorian Doll

*Y*ou are a porcelain Victorian doll in an elderly collector's guest room, and you are tired of it. One night, the Blue Fairy herself visits you. She agrees that it might be time for a change. She offers you two options. You can be a marionette whose movements are totally controlled by the puppet master but at least you know who's in charge and he's not terrible at his craft. Or you can be an automaton who believes he is a human with free will but is afraid of making a bad decision, when in fact everything he does, including believing he is free and feeling his fear, has been programmed by a computer scientist who has long since died. You must decide in one minute or remain a porcelain Victorian doll. What is your choice?

40.

Pass to Narnia

In C. S. Lewis's *The Lion, the Witch, and the Wardrobe*, Lucy is initially drawn to the Professor's wardrobe because of what's hidden inside: fur coats. But the fur transforms into "something hard and rough and even prickly," just like tree branches, and instead of solid wood at the back, distant light. Now delicate flakes fall, and Lucy finds herself in a snowy forest.

But if a wardrobe opens to far-off lands—Arthur Rimbaud remembered his holding a "distant sound, a vague and joyful murmur"—it is also a retreat.

You are a child. Amidst the dark odor of old shoes, winter coats, mothballs, a trace of perfume, you sit and dream of what you dream of, anything, since for once, *total privacy*. In the closet is inmost you.

Make your closet a dream chamber.

First, record the time in your notebook, then walk into the closet and close the door behind you.

Sit comfortably.

Let go of focus and direction, and drift . . . memory, reverie, fantasy . . .

Do this until your back feels cramped or you grow drowsy. Exit the closet. Once more record the time.

How long, clock-wise, were you on the inside? Does this duration correspond to how long it *felt* like you were in the dark? What was your subjective time? Write down the minutes.

Your inner watch almost certainly differed from the actual clock. Is this divergence a negative, a disclosure of the unreality of subjective states, or is it a positive, a revelation of our ability to free ourselves from linear time?

It is likely both at once, this discrepancy: scary and exhilarating. Isn't this the twofold nature of the closet?

Repeat this exercise over the next few weeks. Your goal is to sync your inner clock with the outer. When this happens, briefly describe your feelings. Pay special attention to whether you feel you have gained something or lost.

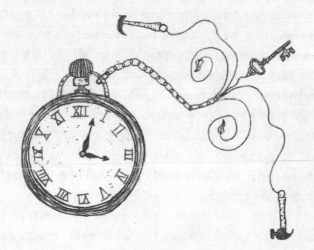

41.

Get from A to Z

*T*o demonstrate that motion is an illusion, Zeno of Elea (495–430 BCE) proposed a paradox.

Achilles and a tortoise agree to a footrace. Since he is fleeter of foot, Achilles grants the tortoise a one-hundred-meter head start.

They're off!

Achilles quickly covers the one hundred meters. Only by the time he does, the tortoise has moved forward, ever so slightly. Achilles makes up the difference, but the turtle has once more progressed, and so the warrior covers that ground. The tortoise, however, has again inched closer to the finish.

Each time the racers progress, Achilles' distance from his competitor decreases by a fraction. But this splitting never ends. Half of ½ is ¼, half of which is ⅛, which divided is ⅟₁₆, and you cut that in half and it's ⅟₃₂, and so on, infinitely. So Achilles cannot overtake the tortoise. He is doomed to trail the animal forever, even if each stride closes the distance.

But while the warrior *mathematically* fails to overtake the tortoise, *empirically* he does. Watch him whiz by the reptile and take the prize.

There are two versions of Achilles, existing simultaneously: the one who prevails once, and the one who fails forever.

If you had to choose, which Achilles would you rather be? The one who wins a hollow race against a vastly inferior opponent and dies not long after, or the one who, to everyone's shock, loses to a turtle, but strides eternally, with who knows what possibilities before him?

What is the reason for your choice? When you have figured it out, your relationship with time will be more intimate, and you will know more pressingly what your death—hopefully a long way off—means to you.

42.

Sacralize the Absurd

*S*ymbols of memento mori—which means "remember death"—are now everywhere. If in the early modern period you could suffer reminders of your mortality in rare paintings of skulls or in occasional skulls on tombstones, clocks, or rings, now you can find the death's-head on scarves, handbags, shot glasses, coffee mugs, key chains, earrings, bracelets, sunglasses, gloves, sneakers, skateboards, dresses, T-shirts, and tattoos.

A once powerful admonition to make your time meaningful has become a stale commodity.

Let's forget about death for a while and remember something just as pervasive and powerful: the *ridiculous*.

Where the memory of death is sorrow turned to wisdom, recall that the ridiculous is sorrow turned *away*. What is sorrow but a realization of the chronic gap between what we want but can't have and what we have but don't want? To transform this feeling of absence into a life lesson is exhausting. Why not just accept that life is rigged against us—we are wired to desire what we can't acquire—and laugh at the trick? Isn't this the essence of comedy, characters striving for dignity but made ridiculous by gravity?

We are the butts of a cosmic joke. Don't be a bad sport. Get in on the laughter. To celebrate silliness is serious sanity. To slip on the peel informs you of grace.

Find an object that reminds you how ludicrous it all is.

Maybe your daughter's crimson marble you stepped on late at night as you shuffled to the bathroom and you felt like your foot bone cracked and when you jerked away, you stumbled into the bookshelf and all your travel souvenirs from Japan crashed down from the top.

Or perhaps that hat you thought made you look so cool but now you realize, not so much. Or the sketch or poem you once believed was genius, or the self-help book that wasn't as salvific as you thought, or a love letter from a botched relationship.

Place this thing by your nightstand or in your work space. Once a day look at it and say to yourself, "It just doesn't matter." Yes, in the end, maybe it does, but for this moment, take a break from your Quest for Meaning and smirk at what fools we mortals are.

43.

Do Nothing

[T]he nothingness of the future had gained a framework-y somethingness that felt privately exciting, like entering a different family's house as a small child, or the beginning elaborations of a science-fiction conceit.

TAO LIN

Legend has it that Bodhidharma, founder of Zen Buddhism, stared at the wall of a cave for nine years. He did this as an extreme act of zazen, seated meditation in which the practitioner lets his thoughts flow without judging or controlling them. Apparently, Bodhidharma dozed off briefly during his seventh year; he grew so angry at his weakness that he sliced off his eyelids. When the flaps of skin reached ground, they grew into tea leaves. From that time on, students of Zen could use tea as a stimulant to keep them alert.

Whether you are a student of Zen or not, staring at a wall is good for you. Doing nothing in particular can actually relieve stress, especially now, when we are bombarded by information. In addition, blanking out, like being bored, encourages innovation;

freed from focusing, the mind can wander into new areas and discover new ideas.

In a quiet room, stare at a wall for ten minutes.

At the end of the period, briefly answer these questions. Did the session seem longer than ten minutes? How much longer? Did you spend a good part of the activity asking yourself, *Why am I doing this activity?* Did you ever feel like you let go of your thoughts and let them flow on their own? Did anything surprise you? Did you learn anything about yourself? Is this an activity you would do again?

Do this exercise at least two more times over the next few days, comparing each experience with earlier ones.

Whatever the outcome, the next time you're doing nothing, you're not doing nothing.

44.

Turn Off the Sound

*W*atch a favorite movie with the sound turned off. List three gestures of the lead actor you didn't notice before. The next week, listen to this same movie without watching it. List three verbal nuances that escaped you earlier. The next time you are in a serious conversation with an intimate, try to see and hear them with the same alertness and clarity.

45.

List Your Top Five Weird Actors

*S*ome actors construct a weird persona to which they remain faithful. Their "weirdness" thus becomes formulaic, and no longer that weird. Actors in this category might be Johnny Depp, Milla Jovovich, and Samuel L. Jackson.

But there are other actors whose strangeness transcends blueprint. Their performances are unpredictable, disquieting, enthralling. These are the truly strange performers.

What five actors would you place in this latter classification? The finalists for my list would include Tilda Swinton, Benicio Del Toro, Forest Whitaker, Uma Thurman, and Harry Dean Stanton.

Once you list your five performers, ask yourself, *What were my criteria?* Your answer will reveal your personal definition of weirdness, which can inform your own behavior.

46.

Cop a Deadpan

*D*eadpan comedy reveals the absurd gap between event and reaction. The stone-faced comedian—Buster Keaton, Bill Murray, Kristen Wiig, Janeane Garofalo, Ronny Chieng—remains impassive before circumstances that cry out for a more passionate response.

The irony inherent in deadpan humor has made it attractive to writers negotiating dangerous extremes. Hemingway's stoically clipped style responds to the inexpressible horrors of World War I, while Joan Didion's similarly understated sentences counter the bizarre occurrences of the late 1960s. More recently Teju Cole's protagonist in *Open City* is straight-faced toward America's racism.

In comedy or fiction, deadpan puts awkward questions to the audience: Are you reacting appropriately to the world? Are you too emotional? Or not sensitive enough?

Choose a day and tell yourself that during at least one conversation you will, when you don't quite know what to say, go stone-faced. Don't give in to the urge to break the silence. Wait to see what happens. How long before someone else speaks? Is the talk nervous? Disdainful? Does anyone comment on your attitude? Does the conversation end quickly or pick up again?

You've created a moment of improvisational theater, in which you and your audience underwent an uncomfortable break in rhythm, and in the pause, asked, *What the hell am I doing?*

47.

Watch Strangers Watch You

*Y*our flight is delayed, you're sick of reading, you're too uncomfortable to sleep, and so you start checking out the crowd. Which characters capture your attention? For the ones that do, you create a past, present, and future out of a few details—hair, clothes, expression, luggage—and this speculative storytelling helps pass the time until your flight departs.

But is someone in the waiting area doing the same to you?

What's your story?

Visit a library or mall or coffee shop or bar—any public place where you can sit comfortably among other people for a while. Take your notebook.

Scan the scene for the person you find most intriguing. Now imagine how you appear to that person.

List five adjectives he would use to describe you.

Based on these descriptors, what story would he construct? What sort of past would a person like you have in his mind? Present? Future?

Briefly write the narrative he might be making to account for you.

Do this activity about once a month. It encourages you to see yourself from a vantage point beyond your own eyes—always a useful check on self-centeredness.

The exercise also urges you to contemplate what you want others to see in you, what you fear others see in you, and how you actually appear to others.

48.

Perform Dorian

*O*scar Wilde's *The Picture of Dorian Gray* (1891) is a tale of uncanny reflection. After an artist captures Dorian's image perfectly, Dorian becomes so enamored of his own beauty that he offers his soul in return for eternal youth. His wish is granted, but with a catch: while his body remains pristine, the painting—stored in an attic—takes on the ugliness of Dorian's sins. It mirrors his hidden interiors.

Rationally, we know that mirrors can only reflect the visible world, but there likely remains a fear—or hope—that the glass might reveal more about us than our features express. The Troxler Effect can support this irrational impulse. In 1804, Ignaz Paul Vital Troxler found that if we fix our gaze on one part of a visual field, the other parts fade. This happens in the mirror: if you stare too long at your eyes, say, the rest of your face blurs and warps. "Those strange fringes aren't my actual face," you might say to yourself. "Maybe they're revelations of feelings I've been hiding."

According to a recent study by Giovanni Caputo, if you stare at your face long enough—seven minutes—you are likely to see more drastic distortions of your face, perhaps even monstrous creatures.

Now you understand the child's game: when you stare in the mirror in a dimly lighted bathroom and repeat "Blood Mary" thirteen times, you're bound to see something that doesn't equal your face.

Write down three adjectives that best describe your current mood.

Now stare at your face in the mirror for seven minutes.

When you are finished, briefly describe what happened: What did you see in the mirror? What were your thoughts and feelings?

Return to the adjectives you wrote down at the outset of the exercise. What is the relationship between them and your mirror session?

Whatever you discovered, you are Dorian near his demise, facing in the glass what you thought no one could see.

49.

Stare at Someone
for a Long Time

*W*hy is staring at another person so much more mesmerizing and disturbing than gazing at your own image?

Staring haunts us. As kids, we stage staring contests. Or we try to stare the bully down. Our parents tell us it's rude to stare. But when we mature, we don't forget that random eye-lock with the stranger on the subway. Was it aggressive or interested? We stare when we require courage: death in the face, into the void. We also stare to express paranoia and suspicion. Nowhere does the duplicity of staring reveal itself more than in our romantic gazing. We want to concentrate all of our love into our eyes; however, we realize that there is a fine line between the erotic gaze and the creepy gawk.

To stare straight into someone's eyes even for ten seconds is intense. But what if you looked into these same eyes for ten minutes?

A recent study by Giovanni Caputo (the same scientist who researched mirror staring) has shown that when people stare into each other's eyes for a long time, they feel as if they are separating from their bodies and time is slowing down. They also might witness their partner's face morph into an animal or a monster, the visage of a relative or friend, or even their own expression.

Caputo thinks the hallucinations might arise from sensory deprivation. When "the brain snaps back to reality after zoning out . . . [it] projects subconscious thoughts onto the face of the other person." If we relate to others by imagining ourselves in them, then an extreme encounter might heighten this process.

This study might benefit schizophrenics, since it sheds light on how hallucinations might occur: as eruptions of subconscious parts of the self into consciousness.

Are there gains for those of relative mental health?

Have a staring contest to find out. Choose your significant other, or a friend, or a workmate or acquaintance, and agree to stare at each other for ten minutes. When you are finished, discuss the experience. Did you feel as though you were disintegrating? How did time feel? What did you hear and see? Animals? Monsters? Did your partner turn into a mirror?

When you are alone again, ask yourself: *Do I feel closer to this person now, or has the relationship grown awkward?* The answer is likely a little of both, and so staring, no matter how hard we try to explain, retains its strange power to attract and repulse.

50.

Visit an Abandoned Building

Perfect order is the forerunner of perfect horror.

CARLOS FUENTES

Tim Edensor, a geography professor, believes that abandoned places attract us because they "offer an escape from excessive order." They are "marginal spaces filled with old and obscure objects. You can see and feel things that you can't in the ordinary world."

Find an abandoned building. Walk around it. Enter, if you can.

Where are the people who lived or worked here and then left for another place, or the grave? What if events had taken a more fortunate turn?

bunting

Take a picture of the wreck. Develop it or print it out and then tape or glue it to a left-hand page in your notebook. On the right-hand page, compose a brief speculative narrative of this building's history and the plight of its last inhabitants.

Reserve nine more pages for similar entries about other abandoned buildings. This part of your notebook might be called "Ruminations on Ruins." If you enjoy these meditations, consider devoting an entire notebook to them.

51.

Pen Obituaries

*I*n "That to Philosophize Is to Learn to Die," sixteenth-century essayist Michel de Montaigne argues that the goal of life is avoiding the fear of death. One way to realize this goal is to make wise use of time. If we squander our hours, we fear death as a killer of possibilities. To die is to regret. But if we fill each day with purposeful activity, we see death as an organic conclusion of a fertile life.

A student of Greek and Roman antiquity, Montaigne knew that Democritus philosophized by hanging out among tombs, and that Stoic Epictetus urged his disciples to think of death every time they kissed a loved one. This correspondence between contemplating death and enjoying a meaningful life later became the basis for a practice pervasive during Europe's early modern period: keep a skull near you to remind you that your soul's state at death decides damnation or redemption.

We need not go to such excesses to grasp how death can energize life. All we require is pen and paper and a willingness to be honest.

If you were to live the life you most desire, how would the world view you after you've died?

To answer this question, imagine your ideal death. How long do you want to have lived? What do you want to have accomplished? What kind of family, if any, would you want to leave behind?

Write the obituary celebrating this life.

This is the north star toward which you should navigate your days.

But what if you died tomorrow? What would the obituary for that death read like? And what if you didn't write it, but a friend did? What about a neutral acquaintance? One of your enemies?

Write a brief obituary of your current self from each of these three perspectives: the friend's, the acquaintance's, the foe's. What do they tell you about your life up until now? What do you want to change?

Maybe nothing, but probably not.

52.

Rub a Tombstone

We all owe death a life.

SALMAN RUSHDIE

$\mathcal{F}$or centuries, corpses rested near churches. They were marked by simple tombstones engraved with skulls and grim sermons for the living—*memento mori, tempus fugit*. But these church graveyards grew overcrowded. Coffins had to be stacked one on top of the other, sometimes six deep, the top corpse only a foot from the surface. The stench sickened, and it harbingered disease.

In the early 1800s, a solution arose: bury people outside the city. So originated the "rural cemetery": the graveyard as an expansive park on whose meandering walkways mourners enjoyed handsome oaks, botanical varieties, and tombs adorned with angels, sleeping children, and flowers. On weekends, picnicking families, idle strollers, and young lovers might join actual mourners among the picturesque paths.

The rural cemetery fostered taphophilia, the love of graveyards. Drawing from the so-called Graveyard Poets of the eighteenth century, Romantic poets like Shelley and Keats—both buried in Rome's sylvan Protestant Cemetery—viewed the graveyard as an invitation to meditate on the mingling of death and beauty.

In *Cemeteries*, Keith Eggener claims that the rural cemetery inspires heightened awareness because its ornate gates lead to an "alternate" city beyond the "mundane world." Within the precincts of the dead, we brood over things the living world ignores, such as time's indifference to individual striving, memory's role as the only stay against erasure, the abundant rot required for even the smallest stalk. And we ask impertinent questions: *Am I wasting my life? Are the dead more interesting than the living? Why am I drawn to skulls?*

For a day, play the taphophile. Your goal is to quicken your consciousness of your own mortality and the importance of those already deceased. A promising technique for achieving this goal is to make a gravestone rubbing.

Secure large sheets of tracing paper and a sharp pencil.

Enter a rural cemetery if you can, but if not, any cemetery that attracts you will serve well.

Walk around until you light upon a tombstone that speaks to you. Maybe you like the shape or the design, or the name of the deceased or the epitaph. Place your paper over the surface of the stone and rub your pencil, lead to the side, over the paper. Hold the paper up to the sky and look at it.

When you get home, put the rubbing in a safe place.

If you found the activity stimulating, do it again. Start a collection: your own book of the dead.

53.

Doodle Around Your Grief

*I*n the middle of a blank white page, write the name of the person who has hurt you the most. Maybe a lover who cheated on you, a friend who betrayed you, a parent who neglected you.

Around this person's name, draw doodles. Do this for ten minutes.

At the end of this time, with pencils or markers, color your patterns. Do this also for ten minutes.

Find a place to hide your piece of abstract art.

Now reflect. How has this creation affected your attitude toward your grief? "Not at all" is a legitimate answer.

Do this exercise, including the reflection, once a month for the next eleven months, each time with a different doodle and color configuration, each time with a different hiding place.

At the end of a year, recover all twelve artworks and lay them out in chronological order.

Write a brief narrative of the development from picture one to picture twelve. What is the main conflict of the story? What is its theme? How does its ending make you feel?

Hopefully, that your pain has lessened. If not, perhaps you at least see it differently, and you can use this altered sight to distance yourself from its ache.

As a reminder of your yearlong journey and as a celebration of your creativity, hang your works on a wall, in their proper sequence.

When you grow tired of looking at them, gather them into a sheaf and bury them at a place blighted by your failed relationship.

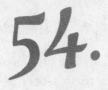

54.

Explore Your Dark Corners

*E*xplore the bottom corners of your dwelling. Gather one artifact from your journey. A dust bunny? A moth wing? A dead ladybug? A cobweb? A pen cap? A marble?

Place the thing in an envelope, write your name on the envelope, and stow the envelope in a drawer you rarely use.

Let time pass.

One day when you are searching for AAA batteries and you open the drawer, you will light upon the envelope. You will open it, and lower into the shadowy nooks in your heart, and accommodate more of life.

55.

Suspend a Pomander

*D*uring the Black Plague, Europeans wore, usually around their necks, pomanders, hollow spheres containing fragrant herbs. Doctors of the time believed (erroneously) that the plague spread through the air, and so lovely odors might repel the sickness.

Eventually pomanders (the name comes from the Old French "pomme d'ambre"—apple of amber—amber being a perfume, ambergris) abstracted into all-purpose talismans. Hence, their roles now at Christmas (oranges spiked with cloves) and weddings (flower balls).

You need a pomander to fight your inmost ailment, be it depression, bipolar disorder, anxiety, OCD, ADHD, grief, nostalgia, petulance, bad mood, too much irony, schadenfreude, jealousy, heartbreak, contempt.

Get a kumquat and watercolors.

On the fruit, paint a face that suits your mood.

Insert cloves to accent the facial features. (The cloves keep the inner fruit from rotting.)

This is your apotropaic charm.

Hang it from your rearview mirror.

56.

Attend Your High Drone

*M*ost sounds quiver to our ears through the air, but the noise of our own voice rides from our vocal cords up through muscle and bone. This conduction makes our talk sound lower to us than to our listeners. When we hear recordings of our voice, we are disturbed by the difference. Who is this speaking in such a high drone?

Hence the uncanniness of hearing your voice recorded. It is yours but isn't. You feel split, as if you are one thing to yourself, but something else to everyone else.

This "voice confrontation" arises not only from differences between sound waves, but also from the tension between familiar and unfamiliar parts of ourselves. The recorded voice reveals emotional nuances—anxieties, angers—we can't detect when we audit our talk raw.

We dislike the *self* of our recorded voice more than the sound. But to listen to our talk as it reverberates outside our bodies can be instructive. We can become more aware of the parts of ourselves we try to hide, and we can grow more expansive, generous, empathetic.

Record yourself reading a favorite passage.

When you play the recording, pretend like the voice isn't yours. Write down three adjectives describing the person the voice implies.

Now read the passage again, without recording it. What three adjectives detail this version? What do they suggest about the owner of the voice, you?

57.

Drop Pennies to Wake Yourself Up

*H*ypnagogia, "leading into sleep," is that limbo between waking and sleeping during which we dream, but know we are dreaming. On this threshold, alpha waves—present when the brain is aware but drifting—and theta waves—markers of the early stages of sleep—combine, and the mind becomes loosely conscious of subconscious currents. This blending of spontaneity and rationality inspires fresh associations, bizarre visions, and startling insights.

Mary Shelley's *Frankenstein* originated in a "waking dream": "I saw—with eyes shut but acute mental vision—I saw the pale student of unhallowed arts kneeling beside the thing he had put together. I saw the hideous phantasm of a man stretched out, and then, on the working of some powerful engine, show signs of life, and stir with an uneasy, half vital motion."

Salvador Dalí napped in a chair with a key between forefinger and thumb. As he relaxed into sleep, the key dropped onto a metal plate on the floor, and half-woke him into his surrealistic visions.

Create your own path to hypnagogia. You might do a variation on Dalí, using a ball bearing or a handful of pennies. You might simply fall asleep sitting up, trusting that the downward jerk of your sleeping head will wake you.

Whatever your technique for inducing hypnagogia, keep a paper and pen beside you. The instant you awaken, write down your thoughts, feelings, and visions.

Do this activity three times a week. Has it sparked your imagination? Given you new ideas? Helped you solve a problem?

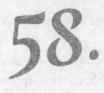

58.

Decide If You Are Asleep or Awake

*O*ne night you dream that a spirit rises from under your bed and tells you that your entire existence is but an episode in a dream of a person who looks exactly like you.

Then in the dream you fall to sleep and dream that a spirit rises from under your bed and tells you that your whole life is simply a scene in the dream of a person who perfectly resembles you.

Then, in this dream within a dream, you wake up.

But are you really awake, or only awake in your dream?

Before you can answer, you fall asleep again.

Then you dream of a spirit who comes through the window and says, the only way you can get good and awake and make it to work on time is to demonstrate the difference between being awake in wakefulness and being awake in a dream. You have three minutes.

How would you respond?

59.

Scry

*Travelers are fantasists, conjurers, seers—and what
they finally discover is that every round object
everywhere is a crystal ball: stone, teapot, the
marvelous globe of the human eye.*

CYNTHIA OZICK

*I*n London's Wellcome Center abides a small round mirror in a sharkskin case. It belonged, so experts believe, to John Dee, the astronomer, mathematician, and all-around occultist who advised Queen Elizabeth and inspired Shakespeare's Prospero.

Dee watched angels in his mirror. They flittered and crossed and whispered of vanished pasts, futures portentous, the tormented now.

Dee was scrying. Stare long enough into a shadowy mirror, an oval of moonstone, a pond, an obsidian shard, and your hidden interiors manifest, and a path clears.

The finding of significant shapes in random flickers is as old as seeing itself, whether the diviner studies animal guts (haruspicy), ant motions (myrmomancy), or the ass (rumpology).

Find a crystal, or perhaps a watch face or knife blade or the surface of an old LP or the glass in a picture frame.

Sit alone with this object in a quiet room. In your notebook, write down a problem in your life. Then stare at the object for nine minutes. At the end of the time, describe what you saw. What did you think about while watching? Do you have a fresh understanding of your problem? Maybe even a plan for what to do next?

If this exercise helped, practice it weekly.

60.

Cast a Magic Circle

*A*bout three thousand years ago, Akkadian magicians performed their rituals within a zisurrû, a circle of flour. It protected them from evil spirits and focused their own powers.

Ever since, the magic circle has proven essential to magical rituals. In Christopher Marlowe's *Doctor Faustus*, the necromancer encloses himself within a circle composed of sacred anagrams and names. Perhaps versed in Marlowe, Victorian artist Henry Gillard Glindoni painted Elizabethan conjurer John Dee surrounded by a circle of skulls. (He later covered the skulls, probably because the commissioner of the piece found them too macabre.)

Gibbous

Wiccans believe that the circle—drawn with chalk, a stick, or a knife—should be nine feet in diameter. Directions and elements can be marked with colored candles: green (North and earth), red (South and fire), yellow (East and air), and blue (West and water). You should leave the circle only through a door you cut with the same tool you used to cast the circumference. To erase the circle, rub it out opposite to the direction of its creation.

In *Homo Ludens: A Study of the Play-Element in Culture* (1938), Johan Huizinga equates the magic circle to sports arenas, theaters, movie houses, and temples. These are places where life's everyday rules are suspended and special ones pertain. Magical rituals and diverting games are, for Huizinga, forms of play, or free activities "standing quite consciously outside 'ordinary' life as being 'not serious,' but at the same time absorbing the player intensely and utterly."

In *Rules of Play: Game Design Fundamentals* (2003), Katie Salen and Eric Zimmerman argue that virtual games should feel like magical circles. When a player enters the game, she leaves her ordinary existence behind and inhabits an alternative world, with its own laws and consequences.

Create your own magic circle. Imagine it less as a paranormal space and more as a psychological one. You can fashion the circle traditionally, with flour or chalk or a stick or a knife, or you could make it out of candles, flowers, drinking glasses, pillows, your favorite books.

Create your circle only in times of stress, when you need to purge yourself of dark powers and absorb healthier ones. Once you are inside your circle, probably sitting (chair, stool, crisscross applesauce), imagine that all obligations have been severed. You are free to think and feel anything you desire.

When you feel refreshed, create a door in your circle and step out, then dismantle your circle in the direction opposite the one by which you made it.

The next time you are downtrodden, repeat.

61.

Cut Your Own Tarot Deck

*I*n the fourteenth century, playing cards migrated from the Mamluk Sultanate to Black Death Europe. The bubonic plague had killed 75 million or more, and the survivors needed distraction. To the Malmuk decks, composed of four suits (Sticks, Coins, Swords, Cups), the Italians added trump cards, which depicted, according to one theory, the Fool's Journey, a vivid story beginning with the Fool and ending with the World.

Tarocchi, whose origin suggests "foolishness," arose from these cards. Seventy-eight cards composed the deck, twenty-two of which were exquisitely painted trumps, including the Fool, the Hanged Man, the Magician, and Death. Players translated these images into narratives about their opponents. These stories were called "destinies."

In eighteenth-century France, "tarocchi" became "tarot," and playful tale-swapping turned occult. But divination lost the essence of the deck: an enchanting interplay between story and chance.

Tarot de Marseilles. Livre de Thoth. Rider—Waite. Fountain. Starchild. Wild Unknown. Mystic Mondays. Robin Wood. Chrysalis.

Deviant Moon, Tattoo, Bleu Cat, Green Witch. These are but some of the scores of tarot decks.

Create your own tarot deck: not for communion with the beyond but for contemplation of the now.

Acquire thin white cardboard.

With a ruler, draw twelve equally sized rectangles.

Use watercolors or colored pencils or pens to create on each rectangle an image you favor: a leaf, a clock, a butterfly, a demon, a tower, a river. Whatever.

Cut out the rectangles.

Arrange the twelve cards into a deck, shuffle. Draw one, place it on a table. Then choose another and put it crosswise on the first.

Say that the first card symbolizes your current situation; the second, your primary obstacle.

Create a story that dramatizes this antagonism.

62.

Master Legerdemain

Two-Drink Mike loves dancing and knows a magic trick. Zero-Drink Mike enjoys biographies and has serious opinions on wildlife. Five-Drink Mike dances with wildlife.

MIKE BIRBIGLIA

*B*etween July and November of 1916, the Allies (the British Empire and the French Third Republic) and the German Empire faced off over the River Somme, located in the north of France. The conflict, later known as the Battle of the Somme, proved one of the bloodiest in history. One million soldiers were killed or wounded, and the British suffered 60,000 casualties in one day. Of those lucky enough to survive, many suffered serious mental damage, then known as shell shock.

Richard Valentine Pitchford was one such soldier. He practiced card tricks to help his recovery. Later, after he became "Cardini," one of the most successful magicians in Europe, he reflected on the therapeutic value of magic: "Of course they [medics] didn't know so much about occupational therapy back in the first World

War, but manipulating my fingers with cards amounted to just that."

Drawing on incidents like these, Charles Folkard, later a famous magician himself, wrote *Tricks for the Trenches and Wards* (1915), a collection of magic tricks meant to cheer up wounded soldiers. Since the publication of Folkard's book, psychologists, teachers, and other magicians have continued to explore the benefits of learning magic tricks. Though the research on the subject isn't conclusive, it does suggest that mastering and performing magic can develop problem-solving skills, cognitive and motor skills, communication capabilities, self-esteem, the imagination, and the ability to tell a good story.

Learn a magic trick and perform it.

Like Cardini, you might choose a card trick: Ambitious Card, Twisting the Aces, Out of this World, Dr. Daley's Last Trick.

But then there is coin legerdemain: Miser's Dream, Empty Cloth, Coin Bite, Three Fly, Elbow Coin Vanish.

Also consider transformation (turning a red scarf yellow), restoration (ripping up a newspaper and putting it back together), or levitation (floating a dollar bill above your hand).

Whatever trick you chose, you will learn a new craft, which will stimulate new thoughts. And when you perform the trick, you will be relating to people in fresh, interesting ways. You will also be *magic*.

63.

Eat Spheroids

*R*esearch has recently shown that people associate round shapes with sweetness. A prime example: some years back Cadbury turned the angular corners of its Dairy Milk bar to rounded ones. Customers complained that the product had changed; it was so sweet that it was sickening. But the recipe had not altered at all.

Conduct your own experiment with roundness and sweetness. You know that spherical shapes affect the tongue, but can they also affect mood? Is it possible that consuming rounded comestibles will put you in a sweeter spirit?

Once a week for a month, spend a day eating nothing but spherical food.

Eggs, beets, oranges, grapes, tomatoes, onions, hush puppies, cheese balls, meatballs, balls of rice, popcorn balls, aniseed balls, gulab jamun, laddu, tapioca pearls, tamarind balls, unni appam, jian dui, melon balls, cherries, kiwis, cantaloupes, scoops of sorbet, honeydews, grapefruits, the caviar of the Kaluga.

At the end of each day, briefly contemplate how this eating has turned your mood, if at all. At the month's close, draw tentative conclusions.

If you find that the food's shape has made you feel better, experiment with other shapes. What can the square inspire, or the triangle?

64.

Fancy a Nook

"Fertile laziness," Baudelaire calls it.

You commit to writing a book. You set a schedule, form an outline, hammer it out. But reverie beckons, and you float into its shimmers and blurs, its peripheries and crossings. Clarity returns. Your sentences flash.

This dance between focus and drift inspires innovation. Those who cultivate daydreaming perform 41 percent better on creative thinking tests than those who simply bear down.

Place a table and chair under a window. Adorn the table with your notebook, a pencil, and a book you admire for its style. Once a day, break from your work and sit there fifteen minutes. Doodle, scribble, sketch, dip into the book, or stare out the window.

Don't try to accomplish anything. Enjoy the languid parataxis of unmanaged time, the "and" and the "and" and the "and."

65.

Carve Soap

*Y*ou hear the brushing of hair or gentle whisperings, or you watch someone fold towels or bake a cake, and a vaguely euphoric tingle begins at the top of your head and gently prickles down your spine. This experience, often relaxing or sleep inducing, is an autonomous sensory meridian response (ASMR).

If you want to feel it, go to the internet. There you'll find over thirteen million videos depicting ASMR triggers, ranging from ordinary activities like a person tapping her fingers or turning the pages of a book to stranger things: someone swallowing octopus sashimi or peeling dried glue.

Apparently the "brain orgasm" caused by these videos can relieve anxiety, depression, stress, and pain. But the positive results of ASMR aren't dependent upon vicarious pleasure. You can undertake the activities yourself.

You can take up, for instance, soap carving, a dependable prompter of ASMR. (The YouTube site ASMR SOAP boasts over 400,000 subscribers.) All you need is a bar of soap (preferably in a color and with a scent you enjoy) and a sharp knife.

Start out by carving leaves, shells, or flowers, before moving to fish, snails, or birds, and then to whatever you fancy.

As you carve, enjoy the soothing repetition of the blade sliding through the soap, the soft fall of the shavings onto the floor, the fine odors. Do this for fifteen minutes a day; you'll feel better, and you'll have charming adornments. And when you get tired of that purple octopus you finished last June, toss it in the bath.

66.

Mix Your Own Color

*I*n the Blombos Cave of South Africa, archaeologists recently discovered a paint-making kit that dates back 100,000 years. It contains grindstones, bone spatulas, hammers, and red and yellow ochre. Near the kit, the scientists found two abalone shells stained with red ochre, bone, and charcoal.

The earliest cave art we know of dates from 45,500 years ago. European and Indonesian caves brim with colors composed of berry juices, blood, minerals, and plants.

Where prehistoric painters mixed their colors with urine, spit, fat, or water, ancient Egyptians bound their pigments—such as the lovely lapis lazuli—with egg. Ancient Greeks and Romans employed beeswax and milk.

Early modern painters used oil for binding. The clarity of their colors enabled them to achieve an unprecedented realism and inspired them to develop new hues such as cochineal (made of crushed insects) and smalt (composed of blue glass).

Some of the most striking colors in the palette originated grimly.

Tyrian purple was distilled from the desiccated hypobranchial glands of mollusks. Once harvested, the glands were dried and boiled. It took about twelve thousand of these snails to color a small piece of fabric.

Ground up mummies, human and feline, composed mummy brown. Pre-Raphaelites loved this purplish rust; it saturates Edward Burne-Jones's melancholy *The Last Sleep of Arthur in Avalon*. When Burne-Jones discovered the macabre origins of the color, however, he buried his tube in his garden.

Indian yellow allegedly came from the urine of cows that had been starved and then forced to eat mango leaves. Their pee was heated into a syrup, dried, and squeezed into chalky clumps of sickly yellow.

Make your own paints. You can easily find recipes that you can vary according to your desire, thus freeing you from the limitations of commercial products. Create colors true to your idiosyncratic vision. Try to find an intimacy with your hues lacking in store-bought paints. After you have stained your fingers, ground the minerals, stirred the pot, you've *earned* the color, and you know it from its insides out.

The recipes for most colors are simple. Take saffron. You empty the white from one egg into a bowl and add half a gram of saffron strands. Let it stand all night, and in the morning, stir. There it is: marigold, goldfish, aurora.

What color will dawn on you?

67.

Make Ink

*F*our thousand years ago, the Chinese made ink from soot and fish. In India, ink-makers burned bones and mixed the ashes with pitch. Europe's standard ink was oak gall, composed of tannic acids and iron salts. With this ink, Da Vinci sketched.

When is the last time you wrote with ink? Probably when you penned a personal note, to sympathize with or thank someone. You put thought into the ink, most likely—the color, certainly, but also the quality.

The thick, alcohol-based ballpoint ink allows for fast drying, but the spread can be uneven—dense here, there light. Lighter fountain pen ink, water based, doesn't dry as quickly; its distribution, however, is likely to be smoother, and you can choose from a variety of inks, such as Sailor Kiwa-Guro black or Waterman serenity blue. The inks of the fountain pen also suggest more intimacy, since the writer's handwriting style shapes the nib that makes the curves and lines.

Writing with ink isn't only more individualized than typewriting; it is also more revelatory. When people write about their feelings for therapeutic purposes, inked remarks are more self-disclosing and beneficial than typed ones. Likewise, to handwrite information is to remember it better, and proficiency in handwriting equals higher literacy skills and cognitive capabilities.

Inspire yourself to ink your thoughts by making your own ink. Here are some possibilities.

Pour boiling water over five bags of black tea. Steep fifteen minutes, then squeeze the bags to get extra strength. Add a teaspoon of gum arabic; stir. Strain until you have a thick paste. This is your ink.

Through a strainer, press half a cup of berries. Blue would be lovely. Add one half teaspoon of vinegar and another of salt. Mix. Now you have ink.

Place ten pennies inside a glass jar. Cover them in vinegar; add a tablespoon of salt. Let the mixture sit for three weeks, stirring twice a day, adding more vinegar as needed. Look at the golden-green-violet-blue. Strain it into smaller glass containers. The ink is ready.

Take a dip pen (you can make one with bamboo, forsythia, or a reed), touch it to the ink you made, and write a letter to someone you love. Describe how it felt to make ink.

68.

Inscribe Your Own Runes

From the third to the sixteenth or seventeenth century runes thrived in Iceland, Greenland, Scandinavia, England, and other countries where Germanic cultures dwelled. The runic alphabet doesn't image cats, ibises, scarabs, eyes, or jackals, like hieroglyphs do. But the letters do retain a pictorial quality, versus Roman script, which marks sound alone. They resemble trees. Google a runestone—there are upwards of 2,500 in Sweden—and you will see carved half-finger-high vertical lines from which smaller lines playfully branch. Crowded side by side in horizontal rows, these letters transform the stone into a dense miniature forest.

Do you fancy trees? More partial to flowers? What about birds or fish?

Choose a flora or fauna. Render it as simply as possible, using only basic geometrical figures—lines, curves, circles, squares, triangles, rectangles.

Draw eight other versions of your animal or plant, each slightly different. Arrange your runes into an interesting pattern. What does it remind you of? This will be the meaning of the word.

Now organize your nine letters into another pattern. What does it look like? Now this word has a meaning.

Repeat this activity seven more times, and you will have nine new words whose meaning is their medium, or nine new shapes that exist simply as (charming) shapes.

Once you open to this odd irony—your runes are words and not words—your figures feel like those classical optical illusions: the rabbit that is the duck, the young woman who is old.

What if you started to look at the whole world this way, as one thing and its opposite? You might be dizzy, but your consciousness would expand, and your perceptions become more generous.

69.

Dream a Game of Surrealism

A poem should go beyond what you already know, and
if it's going to go beyond what you already know, a
poem might say something that begins to have you
question what side you're on, which, in turn, might
begin to have an audience question what side you're on.

JERICHO BROWN

*D*ada, the art movement that thrived in Europe during and just after World War I, got its name, one story goes, when Richard Huelsenbeck inserted a letter opener into a dictionary, and the point lighted on "dada," the French word for "hobbyhorse."

Accident is apt, since Dada artists challenged reason—which justifies war and injustice—through sophisticated nonsense, or what they called "anti-art." Hugo Ball dressed himself in a suit made of blue cardboard, topped by a "high, blue-and-white-striped witch

127

doctor's hat," and recited his poem "Karawane," a seemingly random string of sounds. Hans Arp dropped paper squares of varying colors onto a larger sheet of paper and glued them where they fell. Marcel Duchamp found urinals and bicycle wheels and called them artworks.

As the Dadaist movement disintegrated—aptly, given its aversion to organization—surrealism took its place. Like Dadaism, surrealism celebrated unexpected connections and random eruptions. However, the surrealists, led by André Breton, believed in the power of art to liberate the unconscious. Steeped in Freud, Breton called surrealism "pure psychic automatism," and he developed techniques for nonrational expression, like automatic writing. Of the surrealists, Dalí, depicter of dreams, is the most famous and typical.

The Dadaists and the surrealists created games for liberating the imagination from reason's shackles.

Exquisite corpse. A game involving six or more people. First the group agrees on a sentence structure. Something like "The adjective noun future tense verb the adjective noun." The first person writes an adjective on a sheet of paper and then folds the sheet to hide her word. She passes to the second, who writes a noun that he in turn covers, and so on, until each person has contributed  their assigned part of speech. Then they unfold the paper and behold the sentence. The game's name emerged after surrealists first played it: "The exquisite corpse shall drink the new wine."

How to make a Dadaist poem. Tristan Tzara created this game. Cut an article out of the newspaper, as long as you wish your poem to be.

Then scissor the article into the words composing it and place them in a bag. Shake. Remove the words one by one, writing them down in the order in which they appear. This is your poem.

Decalcomania. In 1936, Óscar Domínguez poured black ink onto white paper and then pressed a blank white sheet of the same size onto the ink. He pulled the top sheet off. The bottom sheet was covered in interesting blobs that Domínguez painted into more recognizable shapes.

Try one of the above games. Or create your own surrealism game.

70.

Lay Off

You are an employee at a factory that produces surrealistic experiences. Your boss says she is going to fire you because you are too real. How will you convince her otherwise?

71.

Save a Nihilist

You successfully persuaded your boss not to fire you. She decided to reassign you instead. You will no longer work in the Hypnagogia department. You will join the Ex Nihilo team, whose task it is to create something out of nothing. You are put in charge of a project to help nihilists, who believe that nothing in this world is valuable, become materialists, those who take satisfaction in things. The best way to start this project is to visit a colony of nihilists living on the island Zemlya Georga. You want to understand the colonists' views but also hope to make them fall in love with one object. You've got to start somewhere, after all. What object will you present to the nihilists and how will you make them adore it?

72.

Press Phosphene into Being

you beat your eyes to
see
The junebug take off backwards.

JAMES DICKEY

*C*lose your eyes for ten seconds. What did you see? Flashes of light, perhaps, or swirling dots and blobs of color, or dancing pixelated forms, or discernible objects, like a pair of lips. Now close again and press gently on your eyelids. Once more for ten seconds. New and more intense colors likely appear, psychedelic and dizzying. You can achieve an equally intense effect when you shut your eyes really hard.

These so-called "closed-eye hallucinations" are caused by biophotonic light, or light that originates from inside the eyes. The optic nerve carries these particles of light to the brain just as it would outside photons, and the brain creates images we can see with our eyes closed. These images are called phosphenes.

Create a phosphene log. Once a day, at the same time, close your eyes for thirty seconds. Once you've opened them, immediately record what you saw. Once you've done this for about a week, ask yourself: Do the same patterns and colors recur, or does the show change from day to day? Does your mood affect the images? What about your level of fatigue?

At the end of a month, draw what conclusions you can. Have these insights revealed to you anything about yourself you didn't already know?

73.

Hear Your Own Ears

There is no such thing as an empty space or an empty time. There is always something to see, something to hear. In fact, try as we may to make a silence, we cannot.

JOHN CAGE

*I*n the spring of 2012, George Michelson Foy entered the anechoic chamber in Minnesota's Orfield Laboratories. He wanted to enjoy the most silent place on earth. Designed to test sound in products like audio equipment or motorcycle engines, Orfield is 99.9 percent sound absorbent. Thick concrete walls and insulated steel ensure that no sound can enter the room, and acoustic fiberglass wedges on the inside mute all echoes. Even footfall is quieted by the suspended netting that serves as a floor, and the absence of lights eradicates the humming of any bulbs.

When the door shut behind Foy, he at first felt a kind of "nirvana, a balm for [his] jangled nerves." He tried to hear anything, but nothing was what he heard. However, he was soon listening to his own breathing, and then his heartbeat, and the rush of blood in his veins. He heard his scalp sliding over his skull and a bizarre metallic scraping noise.

His experience is typical. When the ears are deprived of everyday sounds, they become hypersensitive and detect noises generally drowned out. In addition to what Foy heard, listeners immersed in silence might pick up the hissing of auditory nerves or the stomach's sloshing juices. Some—those with tinnitus—will hear ringing.

On earth there is no silence silent enough to be truly silent. What about outer space? It turns out that ionized gas fills the universe, even vacuums and black holes, and this plasma carries sound. Lightning rushing through this plasma makes a whistling sound, and the Van Allen radiation belt sounds like birdsong.

Find the quietest place you can.

Sit for five minutes. What sounds do you hear? Write them down.

Now sit for another five. Are you picking up on other sounds? Are any of these sounds new to you?

Once more, sit for five minutes. Note fresh noises. Can you now hear things you thought were undetectable, like processes within your own skin?

Continue this exercise until you feel you've heard all you can.

Repeat a week later, in the same place.

Are there similarities with your earlier experience? Differences?

Your goal is to sense worlds heretofore silent and to wonder what the sensations tell you about yourself.

74.

Taxonomize Silence

*N*ot all silences are the same. The silence of an empty building is not the quiet of a desert, which is not like a lonely room or a temple or a faraway forest.

List three experiences notable for their silence. Connect each to an adjective, a color, a memory, and a category.

Here is an example:

I. Soon after Covid-19 broke out, I climbed Rich Mountain in Blowing Rock, NC. The day was wet, and I saw no one on the trail. When I reached the summit, I heard nothing, save, once, a crow a long way off.

ADJECTIVE: Precarious.

COLOR: Gun-Metal Gray.

MEMORY: I first did this hike in the early days of my courtship of a woman I divorced not one year ago.

CATEGORY: A nervy silence.

Once you finish this exercise, gather others. Continue to build your taxonomy. It will quicken your listening.

75.

Anatomize Something

I learned to make my mind large, as the universe is
large, so that there is room for paradoxes.

MAXINE HONG KINGSTON

In an 1851 letter to his father-in-law, Lemuel Shaw, Melville con-
fessed that he wanted to write "those sort of books which are
said to 'fail.'" He meant that he aspired to create great literature,
which would likely be disparaged by a superficial American reader-
ship. But Melville was also describing the essential quality of a
brilliant work: in attempting to describe what can't be described—
the sublimity of the sea, the heart's inscrutability—the book dooms
itself to a kind of failure. This faltering, though, is paradoxically a
success, since language pushed to its limits is robust, heteroge-
neous, superabundant.

That Melville chose to write his most ambitious book—*Moby-
Dick*—in the form of a literary anatomy is apt. This type of
anatomy—distinguished from a medical one—explores an inex-
haustibly compelling subject from a bewildering multitude of perspectives. The anatomy's voluminous interpretive frames suggest

the possibility of complete knowledge; the bottomless topic, how-ever, reminds us that knowing is never finished.

Outside of *Moby-Dick*, a prodigious effort to understand the un-fathomable whale, the most famous anatomy is Robert Burton's *The Anatomy of Melancholy*, first published in 1621. In this book, which eventually ran to over one thousand pages, Burton examines melan-choly from countless angles, including those of philosophy, religion, literature, myth, medicine, folklore, superstition, and personal expe-rience. Like Melville, he fashions a style as superabundant as his sub-ject; for instance, "The tower of Babel never yielded such confusion of tongues, as the chaos of melancholy doth variety of symptoms. There is in all melancholy *similtudo dissimilis*, like men's faces, a disagreeing likeness still; and as in a river we swim in the same place, though not in the same numerical water; as the same instrument affords several lessons, so the same disease yields diversity of symptoms."

To experience the vertigo of trying to fill infinity, make your own anatomy.

Write an interesting feeling on the top of a page. Now compose ten sentences, each of which addresses the feeling from a different perspective.

I'll give you an example.

WEIRD
1. "The whole world's wild at heart and weird on top," Lula says in David Lynch's *Wild at Heart*.
2. How spooky young Elvis is when he sings of a milk cow.
3. Petrichor, that smell of summer pavement just after a rain.
4. That longing for a place that doesn't even exist, like *The Well at the World's End*.
5. And so on and so on and so on.

Now your turn . . .

76.

Identify with Your Hydrogen

We do not grow absolutely, chronologically. We grow
sometimes in one dimension, and not in another,
unevenly. . . . We grow partially. We are relative.
We are mature in one realm, childish in another.
The past, present, and future mingle and pull us
backward, forward, or fix us in the present.
We are made up of layers, cells, constellations.

ANAÏS NIN

It is your birthday, and so you can confidently (and hopefully, happily) say, "I am thirty-five years old." Accuracy is on your side—you have a birth certificate (somewhere)—and also a sense of ownership: the only things I know I possess for sure are the experiences and memories of this particular body.

But what about those days, less happy, when you don't want to possess your identity, when you are sick of it, want to be someone else or nothing at all? Those days, it's helpful to remember that even when you feel most yourself, a unit irrevocably determined by your personal past, you are, temporally speaking, *not* yourself. You are something that's been around forever.

The atoms in your body are billions of years old; hydrogen, for instance, is 13.7 billion years old.

The molecules in the water you drink are 4.5 billion years old, more ancient than the sun.

Your cells might date back only to your birth, but cells in general reach back 3.8 billion years. Same with your breathing; you have been doing so for thirty-five years, but the planet has been panting for 2.5 billion.

Sight started 600 million years back; consciousness, 500 million; language, 150,000.

Imagine yourself as a simultaneity of time frames. Atomically you are, literally, billions of years old. Your molecules and cells connect you with entities that have likewise existed for billions of years. When you breathe, you participate in another billions-of-years-old phenomenon. Seeing and thinking: these pull you back millions of years. Speaking makes you at least 150,000 years old.

Don't fret over an approaching deadline or your dinner party faux pas: you've already lived through untold stresses and gaffs and you'll persist through billions more. From your hydrogen's perspective, none of this matters. Even your deepest griefs seem insignificant when measured against how long people have been lamenting.

This is not to say that your sorrows, or your deadlines or embarrassments, are inconsequential. But you have a temporary respite from the vexation. As though in a time machine, you can rush to a far-flung past where none of your stuff means anything and relax in the indifference before returning, rested and flexible.

Draw a temporal map of yourself. Sketch a human body lying

on its back—crudely or finely, according to ability or gumption. Within the body, draw areas associated with different time frames. Here is the atomic region. Here is sight. Here, speech.

When you wish you had more time, visit the country that has time to spare.

Distort Time

*C*limb a mountain—Mount Marcy, say, up in the Adirondacks—and place a clock at the peak. Next day, drive to the coast—Jones Beach?—and put a clock there. Wait ten years. You'll find that time up in the clouds has moved a hair faster than at the beach, something like 30 millionths of a second faster. You'll age more rapidly in the mountains because the heavier gravity near the coast slows time down.

But we don't require Einstein's theory of general relativity to demonstrate the effect of location on time; we can explore our own interiors. If you are thrown into a life-or-death situation, adrenaline quickens your inner clock, and the world outside your skin seems to slow down. At the other extreme, post-traumatic time appears to stop. You continually relive the pain, obliterating the present and the future. As psychiatrist Robert D. Stolorow puts it, you are "freeze-framed."

We need not suffer extremes to alter temporality. If you were forced to trade in your computer for an older one, you'd find the delay between double-clicking on a file and its opening to be, relatively speaking, slow. But you would eventually adapt to the delay, and the opening would seem instantaneous. Researchers call this process "intentional binding," and they wonder if a feeling of ownership over a process can quicken time.

Simple shifts in attention can also distort time. If we continually look at the clock, then time is sluggish. But when you don't worry about the ticking, so immersed you are in an activity, time accelerates.

Distort time.

Speed it up. Throw yourself into an enterprise you love—tennis, baking, painting, sex—and fifteen minutes feel like five. You are so in sync with the present that you stop looking backward with nostalgia or regret, or forward with anticipation or fear. Time loses its rub. This is eternity: not infinite duration, but intense ephemera.

Now slow it down. Instead of relaxing into an effortless practice, pay attention to an unfamiliar object. Note it minutely, inch by inch. How does it relate to your past? How might it affect your future? After this exertion, look at the clock. Five minutes have seemed fifteen.

What have you learned?

First, the world inside your skull and the one without run at different speeds, and this is disconcerting, since you can never quite tell which clock is correct.

Second, this disturbing gap can be exhilarating, an invitation to shape time to suit your mood, and so feel free, however briefly, of painful hours.

78.

Collect Toadstools

*Attend to mushrooms and all other things will
answer up.*

A. R. AMMONS

Dead man's fingers, poison pie, lead poisoner, Destroying Angel,
death cap, devil's urn.

Don't eat the mushrooms!

Why not?

Bulbous honey fungus, purple jellydisc, dewdrop dapperling,
Drumstick Truffleclub, Plums and Custard.

Whether mushrooms kill you or lift you, they feel preternatu-
ral. You wake up one morning, there they are, in your yard. They
weren't here last night. Where did they come from? Next morning,
they're gone.

Shakespeare's magus Prospero claimed it was the elves' pas-
time to "make midnight mushrooms." When mushrooms arise in
rings, fairies have been afoot. Beware stepping into their circle. A
portal to the faerie realm might open, and you'll fall through and
never return.

In Germany, the mushroom ring is a Hexenkreis, "witches circle," the track left by the coven's dance in the round. The Dutch thought that Satan's milk churn created the circuit.

In the dictionary, "mushroom" comes just before "music." John Cage loved this. Part of his income came from selling rare mushrooms to posh Manhattan restaurants. David W. Rose claims that "the mycological and musical are revealed by Cage as parallel universes."

Another peculiar correspondence is between the red-and-white fly agaric, a highly hallucinogenic mushroom, and the costume of Santa Claus. On the winter solstice, the shaman among the Sámi people of Lapland would ingest fly agaric and embark on a spiritual journey to the tree of life. Located near the north star, this tree offered solutions to the problems of the villagers. When the shaman returned, he distributed these fixes to his people. He wore his mushroom-colored suit and rode mushroom-fueled reindeer. Some believe this hallucinogenic odyssey evolved into the tale of the current Claus.

Lewis Carroll understood the wonders of fly agaric. Before imagining Alice's head trip, he read Mordecai Cubitt Cooke's *The Seven Sisters of Sleep*, which details the effects of eating the mushroom: "Erroneous impressions of size and distance are common occurrences . . . a straw lying in the road becomes a formidable object, to overcome."

This is Alice's problem as she eats one side or the other of the Caterpillar's massive mushroom: finding the right fit.

What mushrooms sync your psyche?

Either through research or walking about, find three mushrooms that interest you. Maybe you like their shape or color, or how they function in their environment, or their nutritional qualities, or their poisonous ones, or how they alter perception.

(Warning: Don't try eating them. Your goal is simply to research and notice.)

In your notebook, paste or draw a picture of the mushroom on the left-hand page and on the right-hand one, answer three questions: What is the most striking characteristic of this mushroom? What is its most interesting fact? What does my attraction to it say about me?

After completing this activity for all three of your mushrooms, you have a fungal mirror of your interiors.

Add more shrooms: more mirrors, more wonder.

79.

Kick Over a Log

*H*omer's Odysseus descends into the underworld to discover his destiny, as does Virgil's Aeneas. Orpheus goes down to Hades to recover Eurydice. Persephone is abducted to the underworld, and Adonis spends the dark half of the year there.

In Catholicism, Jesus between his death and resurrection harrows hell, saving from its fires the righteous who lived before his coming. Dante in his *Divine Comedy* travels through the circles of hell on his way to purgatory and paradise.

Analogous to these lowerings into disorienting darkness are Luke Skywalker braving the murky waters of the Empire's trash compactor, Frodo struggling through the mines of Moria, Alice falling through a rabbit hole to Wonderland, Coraline discovering the Other World.

These journeys depict a crisis in the hero's life, from which she emerges reborn. According to Carl Jung, each of us experiences our own such crisis when we fall into depression. If we heed the sorrow as a call to recover energies we have neglected, we can emerge as heroes of our own psyche.

So—don't be afraid to look underneath. The bed, the stairs, the porch, the rug, the bridge, rocks, old logs. Maybe you can find stuff under there more interesting and valuable than what you see in the light.

Explore an underneath place. You might start by turning over an old log. Record what you see. Probably grubs, pill bugs, ants, earthworms, millipedes, a salamander if you're lucky.

Now look under something else. Perhaps a rock. Again record what you find.

Once more, examine a dark space. What about your couch or bed? Do you spy objects you thought had gone forever? List them.

You've studied three underworlds in micro. Now look at what you think you know about yourself.

80.

Sniff Play-Doh

*I could be bounded in a nutshell and count myself a
king of infinite space.*

WILLIAM SHAKESPEARE

*T*he Smell and Taste Research Center recently showed that smelling a green apple makes a place feel bigger. Perhaps the apple's association with well-being alleviates anxiety and claustrophobia.

Recall an odor you loved when you were a child. Play-Doh? Crayons? Elmer's Glue? Bacon? Small engine oil? Woodsmoke?

Find this smell. As you inhale it, what memory rises in your mind? Record it.

Try to remember other favorite smells. Recreate them, sniff them, describe what memories they evoke.

When you are stressed, return to these entries in your notebook. They will remind you of a better time, and they will lighten your breathing, if only for a minute.

81.

Look Up

*A*ccording to neuroscientist Fred Previc, one of our brain's visual networks centers on the interpersonal encounters of the ground level. Another system, though, directs above the horizon, toward "extrapersonal space." When stretching to distant heights, the brain behaves as it does when it experiences religious awakening, contemplative insights, and imaginative leaps. That transcendent states often involve the raising of the eyes is apt.

At least three times a day, force yourself to look up—to a flag-pole's finial, the top of a tree line, the roof's pitch, the church's spire, the center of a high ceiling, the radio tower's antenna, the apex of a tall building, the drifting clouds, the very sun.

Hold your gaze on the elevation for a minimum of one minute. You might not become one with the infinite, but you will give your mind the feeling of "more," and after a day of "enough," this can feel divine.

82.

Build a Model of Your Foot

Break a vase, and the love that reassembles the
fragments is stronger than that love which took its
symmetry for granted when it was whole.

DEREK WALCOTT

*I*f you lived in ancient Greece and you suffered from an infected foot, you would visit the local temple of Asclepius, the god of medicine, and you would soon find yourself in the abaton, or the healing room. There you would sleep the night—your time of incubation—hoping that Asclepius would visit you, either in a dream advising a particular treatment or by performing an actual medical procedure.

To coax the god into applying to your foot his very finest skills, you would have brought along a stone replica of your sick appendage. This votive would also serve as a token of appreciation.

The votive was essential to ancient medicine. At the site of Asclepius's temple in Corinth, archaeologists have discovered votives of arms, hands, legs, and feet. The reason for this predominance is that many of the supplicants were farmers from rural areas near the city; as workers of the land, they would have been susceptible to injuries to their limbs. But Corinth proper was a port city infamous for its prostitution, and its venereal diseases. This accounts for the many penis-shaped votives also found in the temple.

What ails you, inside or out? Physically or emotionally? Create a votive in the form of your disorder. You can do this with modeling clay or Play-Doh, or you can draw a picture.

If you are suffering from a sore knee or an irritable stomach, the replication is easy enough: render the anatomy. But if you are grieving or depressed, the mimicking is less direct; you must resort to abstraction. Is your sorrow sharp, like a blade, or is it dull, a kind of festering blob?

Once you have completed your votive, take it to your favorite tree. Hold it up to the branches and imagine how you would feel right now if you were free of your ailment. Now bury your votive just below the surface of the earth.

Go home. Hope that as your votive decays in the soil, so will your pain dissolve.

83.

Seed a Wasteland

Cities produce love and yet feel none. A strange thing
when you think about it, but perhaps fitting. Cities
need that love more than most of us care to imagine.
Cities, after all, for all their massiveness, all their
there-ness, are acutely vulnerable.

JUNOT DÍAZ

*T*he uses of nature are clear. *This* habitat is essential to the survival of *this* species. The meadow adjacent to the forest is home to bees and field mice and hawks, little bluestem and troublesome sedge and foxglove.

But the cities are different. Some spaces, such as vacant lots and abandoned houses, appear to have no use at all, other than reminding us of what inhabitants, human or otherwise, once lived there.

Scientists now explore potential uses of so-called urban wastelands. How can humans create city environments that foster natural and emotional vitality? One successful technique is the planting of wildflowers. Creatures hitherto absent from the blank spaces now thrive, and humans enjoy the color and gusto.

Find a vacant lot, or an untended yard of a house for sale, or a strip of grass near a mall, or the median of a highway.

Just before morning or just after dark, in the late fall or early spring, carry to the spot a garden shovel, two twenty-ounce bottles of water, and a mix of wildflower seeds.

(Make sure the seeds will produce local flora, and not be invasive.)

Purple coneflower, orange California poppy, perennial lupine, Lemon Queen sunflower, crimson clover, baby blue eyes, red corn poppy, sweet alyssum.

Till a three-by-three area, scatter the seeds, cover them with dirt, water them.

When they grow, if they do, pass by them once a week.

Don't tell anyone how they got there.

Compose Your Own
Atlas Obscura

It didn't take me long to learn that the discipline or
practice of writing these essays [on delight]
occasioned a kind of delight radar. Or maybe it was
more like the development of a delight muscle.
Something that implies that the more you study
delight, the more delight there is to study.

ROSS GAY

Athanasius Kircher, whom we met in his Wunderkammer, is the main inspiration for *Atlas Obscura*, an internet magazine and touring company that imagines the world itself as an immense cabinet of curiosities.

Launched by Joshua Foer and Dylan Thuras in 2009, the website now describes 18,000 "wondrous and curious places." These range from oddities hidden within everyday locations (a 1,611-foot tunnel under the intersection of Brooklyn's Atlantic Avenue and Court Street), to out-of-the-way museums (Wisconsin's House on the Rock, exhibiting the largest carousel in the world, which contains 269 animals, 182 lanterns, and 20,000 lights), to out-and-out sci-fi eeriness (the Buzludzha Monument commemorating communism, a huge saucer-shaped structure abandoned in the Bulgarian mountains).

Create your own *Atlas Obscura*.

What places in your daily routine are strange? Did you travel to any bizarre locales when you were a child? What about as an adult?

In your notebook, briefly describe each odd place you've already visited. Make sure you explain why the site is curious.

Now your goal is to find more wondrous locations for your atlas. As you make your daily rounds, be alert for odd phenomena. They don't have to be big. A splotch on concrete, a knot on a tree, a mangled rusty rod of metal. But big works, too. Puce water tanks atop old buildings. Smokestacks tilted over empty factories. Rotted-out bridges near collapse.

What matters is, is the site uncanny?

As you search, you will probably find what Ross Gay discovered in scanning daily for a delight: the more you look for strangeness, the more likely you will develop a "strangeness" radar. The more you brood on the strange, the more strangeness there is to brood upon.

85.

Speak "Takete"

*I*n a 1929 experiment, Wolfgang Köhler showed participants a jagged shape and a rounded one, and he informed them that they could call one shape "baluba," and the other "takete." The subjects consistently paired "baluba" with the rounded form, and "takete" with the sharper.

Researchers have since concluded that orbicular shapes activate sounds that round the mouth, while spiky forms straighten lips and tongues.

Take a thirty-minute walk, notebook in hand. Write down five adjectives that describe your experience.

Back home, draw a shape that corresponds to each word.

What smell goes with each shape? And these smells, how do they feel? If you could taste them, how would they flavor your tongue?

86.

Form a Word That *Is* What It Means

I hear bravuras of birds, bustle of growing wheat,
gossip of flames, clack of sticks cooking my meals.

WALT WHITMAN

To get your words as close as possible to your core, save them from semantics. Turn them into objects.

Ralph Waldo Emerson believed that "in good writing, words become one with things." For instance, a "rhyme in one of our sonnets should not be less pleasing than the iterated nodes of a seashell," and an ode should feel like "tempest."

There are several techniques that drive words nearer to things. Most obviously—and this is what Emerson seems to have in mind— there is rhetoric: the effect of the words resembles the impact of a natural phenomenon. Another is the shape poem, whose form on the page figures its subject matter; George Herbert's poem "The Altar" is formed like an altar. And then there are ideogrammatic languages—picture languages—such as Chinese characters and Egyptian hieroglyphs.

But a more readily available, and more immediate, way to collapse word and thing is through onomatopoeia: creating a word whose sound and meaning are the same.

Clack, clunk, bark, whoosh, whish, slither, pitter-patter, murmur, oink, ribbit, kerplunk, hiss, quack, purr.

Silence your home, and sit quietly within it, and listen to the sounds coming from without (cars and wind) and from within (creaks and drips) and write down the letters that capture the most compelling noise. For instance, a squeaking wooden floor could be "wrint," and metal scraping asphalt might be "chich."

What is your onomatopoeia? How many of them can you create? Try to make ten, and then combine them into a euphonic pattern. This is your poem. It signifies through sound, not semantics.

Hum it. Make up a dance that corresponds to its rhythms.

87.

Paint Stones

Secure eight rocks, smooth, size of your fist.

In red, paint a direction on each, such as:

    Floss the back.

    Chew enough.

    Remember kelp.

    Look once.

    Pay half.

    Compare nine.

    Parse the frog.

    Stir the cochineal.

Secretly leave the stones in the yards of friends or strangers.

88.

Be a Prophet

A crazed angel visited you last night and commanded you to compose a gospel of weirdness. Essential to the good news, she proclaimed, are the ten commandments of weirdness. Write these commandments down.

89.

Swerve

A straight line is comforting—predictable and continuous. It is also repetition, stasis: a sign of death. Random swerves from the line are scary, as all randomness is. How can you count on anything? But sudden deviations bring newness into the world. Between the regularity of the line and the chaos of the swerve is the spiral—regular, its form is geometrically stable, and turbulent, its whorls intimate infinite vertigo.

Line, swerve, spiral: the Roman poet Lucretius (c. 99–55 BCE) envisioned this sequence as the progression of all creation. In *De Rerum Natura, On the Nature of Things,* he claims that in the beginning there were only lines, atoms falling in a void. Mars, who loves death, favored this monotonous descent. But Venus, life force, jostled the particles whimsically, swerving them from their paths. The curves she created curled into vortices, gatherings of atoms into turbulent patterns. These eddies were the first living things, and all creatures, including us, remain vortices, integrities through which boundless energies perpetually rush: electromagnetism, water, oxygen.

Bend your Martial routines, surround yourself in Venusian eddies.

Draw a spiral and hang it on your wall. Acquire a nautilus for your desk. Place a short coil of rope beside your bed. Hang a picture of a tornado. Look at an open rose.

Each morning study your spiral and say, "I will veer from my normal path today."

You might eat something new for breakfast or say something surprising to your loved ones. If you walk to work, take a different route; if you drive, do the same. At work, speak to a colleague you've ignored. Have something different for lunch. Sign up for a music class. Take a course in Spanish. Close your eyes, point to a world map, and take a vacation to the spot you're pointing to.

90.

Play the Flâneur

*Not to find one's way around a city does not mean
much. But to lose one's way in a city, as one loses one's
way in a forest, requires some schooling.*

WALTER BENJAMIN

*P*ut away your phone, stuff a daypack with water and snacks.
Take a bus or train to an unfamiliar stop and hike your way back
home. Or simply walk from home until you are in new terrain.

The point is, get lost. And stay that way. At least for a while.
You want to walk just to walk, with no other purpose than to wander through newness.

You are playing the flâneur, a "voyeuristic stroller," as Susan
Sontag puts it, "who discovers the city as a landscape of voluptuous
extremes."

This role arose during the nineteenth century, when pop
ulations in Paris and London increased prodigiously, and every
labyrinthine turn promised strange adventures. For Charles Baudelaire, to meander among the throng was to be a poet, "a kaleido-
scope gifted with consciousness, responding to each one of its

movements and reproducing the multiplicity of life and the flickering grace of all the elements of life." Virginia Woolf, flâneuse, relished how rambling freed her from the rounds of her rooms. When we emerge into the streets, the "shell-like covering which our souls have excreted to house themselves, to make for themselves a shape distinct from others, is broken, and there is left of all these wrinkles and roughnesses a central oyster of perceptiveness, an enormous eye."

Easing into your own unmapped drift—which thrills in small towns as much as large cities—enjoy your freedom from practicality, which locks you into cause and effect—*if* I speed up here, *then* I can get to work on time—and alienates you from the now, which is all that is alive.

Save the moment from the ticking. Trade the causal for the casual. Though physically lost, you will find fresh feelings, and an odd home among the foreign.

When you return to your abode, choose a song that captures the mood of wandering in a strange terrain. Listen to the song and then, in your notebook, list it under the heading "Drift Songs." Over time, as you undertake more excursions, expand your list.

toooost

91.

Take Your Turn

*C*reate your own "how to be weird" exercise.

92.

Glance Askance

*A*ccording to Ralph Waldo Emerson's youngest son, Edward, Thoreau once said of nature, "She must not be looked at directly, but askance, or by flashes: like the head of the Gorgon Medusa, she turns the men of Science to stone."

When you look at an object head-on, you seek its center, its essence. But this direct gaze blinds you to interesting edges, blurs, mergers. These peripheral regions captivated Thoreau. They inspire reverie, poetry, mystery.

Go outside. Find something that interests you—a stalk of ragweed, maybe, or a discarded green bottle. Now stare at it head-on for a minute. Record what you notice. Now do the same thing but shift your attention to your peripheral vision. What details has this new emphasis revealed? Now look away from the thing and slowly turn your gaze back to it. Do this three times. Again, what have you detected?

Perhaps this: the *focus* your teachers so adamantly urged is only half of learning.

93.

Perform the Percy Switcheroo

According to Walker Percy in his essay "Loss of Creature" (1954), most biology students don't see the frog they dissect. Unlike the idler who at the pond's edge happens upon a springing greenish-brown blur, the student is benighted by the "symbolic package" that reduces the amphibian to an "example of" the principles of anatomy. The particular frog is lost; only the idea remains.

The same is true of a sonnet. If I discover a Shakespeare poem of this type out in the woods, and I read it over, I enjoy the specificity of the verse, its strange "is-ness." But in a classroom, I experience the poem as an instance of a concept.

Outside of finding a pond frog or studying a forest sonnet, one way to recover the "creature" from its symbolic packaging is to defamiliarize the educational setting. What if a biology professor brought a sonnet to class, or if an English teacher supplied her students with scalpels and dead frogs? Then students could encounter the words and the organs in all of their luminous charm.

Let's call this substitution of one subject matter for another the "Percy Switcheroo." Why not do your own?

Start small. If you normally drink coffee, have hot tea one

morning. If you are a morning person, try accomplishing an important task late at night. Are you a regular reader of genre fiction? Then peruse some articles on *Scientific American*.

Then graduate to more elaborate reversals. Are you a chatty type? Then spend a day saying little. If you exercise a lot, take a day sitting around.

In all of these cases, the Percy Switcheroo will *italicize* your experience—make it emphatic, immediate, memorable.

94.

Spend a Day as a Termite

*I*mportant films, art films, films espousing a noble cause: these kinds of pictures (typically nominated for Academy Awards for Best Picture) share cogency (their action conforms to an overall moral); continuity (all events fit into a linear narrative); and conspicuous creativity (the screen is replete with prizewinning effects).

For Manny Farber in his 1962 essay "White Elephant Art and Termite Art," such cinema is "reminiscent of the enameled tobacco humidors and wooden lawn ponies bought at white elephant auctions decades ago." It is stiff, unwieldy, gilded: less about life, more about its own preciousness.

Opposed to this bloat is what Farber calls "termite art," works that "seem to have no ambitions towards gilt culture but are involved in a kind of squandering-beaverish endeavor that isn't anywhere or for anything." Peculiarly, "termite-tapeworm-fungus-moss art . . . goes always forward eating its own boundaries, and, likely as not, leaves nothing in its path other than the signs of eager, industrious, unkempt activity." Directors of termite films—sometimes B pictures—are more interested in play than meaning. Howard

Hawks's *The Big Sleep*, for instance, appears to exist only to keep Bogart and Bacall engaged in sexy badinage. Likewise, the films of Laurel and Hardy have no purpose beyond humorous knockabout.

Farber believes that the consummate termite actor is John Wayne, who in *The Man Who Shot Liberty Valence* focuses on "how to sit in a chair leaned against the wall." Contemporary actors who share Wayne's attention to the present are, I believe, Brad Pitt (watch him fix a TV antenna in *Once Upon a Time in Hollywood*) and Greta Gerwig (watch her run through New York City in *Frances Ha*).

Spend a day as a termite. Days you aren't working for money are best for this. In the midst of whatever you're doing, if you become interested in something else, do it, and then if something else comes up, follow that whim, and so on, until it's difficult to remember where it all started. The day should become so digressive that the distinction between focus and digression disappears.

When you do return to "meaningful" activity—gainful employment—retain the termite spirit. Whenever you have the chance, focus on captivating details and forget your grand purpose.

Hopefully, your days will morph into dynamic conversations between spontaneity and discipline, in which the limitations of both vanish and the virtues intensify.

95.

Frequent a Shoreline

*I*n the *Enuma Elish*, an ancient Babylonian creation myth, all life springs from Tiamat, the mighty ocean. Drawing from this tale, the authors of Genesis imagined the primal chaos as liquid; God formed this turbulence into the universe.

If the sea symbolizes origin, the lake represents harmony. In Arthurian legend, the Lady of the Lake's Excalibur heals a war-torn land. The West Lake in Chinese myth is a jade ball from heaven; wherever it shines, earth grows flowers.

Unlike lakes, rivers flow; they are time's growth and decay. The Ganges accepts the dead and purifies the living. The River Styx connects the breathing world with the realm of shades.

Water has figured prominently in major literary works, spanning from Homer's *Odyssey* to Derek Walcott's *Omeros*. American literature alone is imminently liquid. In Toni Morrison's *Beloved*, the Ohio River carries Sethe to freedom. Langston Hughes's "The

Negro Speaks of Rivers" imagines old African rivers flowing into the poet's veins. Thoreau's *Walden* celebrates a seemingly bottomless lake. Melville in *Moby-Dick* broods over the sea's terror and ecstasy.

Recently, psychologists have realized that the imaginative writers are right: water isn't simply required for physical life. As liberation, strength, depth, and sublimity, it is also essential to psychological well-being.

In 2011, cognitive scientists randomly texted 60,000 respondents questions about their moods throughout one day. Those dwelling near water scored six points higher on a scale of happiness than those living in drier regions.

Another study has demonstrated the "blue-mind effect." To immerse yourself in water is to slow your neurochemicals to stress levels close to those achieved by meditation.

It turns out that one need not even be near water to enjoy its benefits. Simply imagining an awe-inspiring experience of water can encourage more ethical behavior, and watching a video about water can reduce chronic pain.

Create your own aqueous therapy.

Find a body of water near you. It doesn't have to be an ocean, lake, or river. You can choose a pond, creek, spring, reservoir, canal, marsh, rill, even a large puddle.

Every other day for a month, visit the water. Look for differences. On the bank, are there changes in greenery, the rocks, wildlife, the amount of litter? In the water proper, do you notice alterations in level, color, creatures? What about the horizon? The sky?

Record your observations in your notebook.

At the end of the month, answer these questions:

What are the primary changes I noticed?

How have my visitations to this aquatic place affected my moods?

If I were to recommend this activity to a friend, what would I say?

Once you answer this last question, you'll know whether water assuages your melancholy or simply keeps you hydrated.

96.

Manufacture a Portable Door

*I*n *The Marriage of Heaven and Hell*, from 1790, William Blake announces "If the doors of perception were cleansed every thing would appear to man as it is, Infinite."

Since most of us perceive only what threatens us or supports us, we divorce ourselves from things as they really are. If they don't scare us or pleasure us, they might as well not exist. All we really see is ourselves: world as mirror of our preoccupations.

But sometimes curiosity or wonder flings us beyond our egos and our eyes open, like doors, to the cosmos as it is: intricate, nuanced, subtle, abundant, magnificent—infinitely spirited.

Cleanse your doors of perception.

Take a piece of paper, 8 x 11. Cut out a 5 x 7 section. Around the edges of this section, draw a frame, about half an inch wide. Color it however you wish. Cut out the blank part.

This frame is your doorframe. Gaze through it. Give whatever you see your full attention. Notice everything about it you can—color, shape, texture, how it captures the light, where it is shadowed, anything.

Record what you noticed about this object.

Fold your frame up, put it in your wallet or purse or pack, and carry it around like you would a magnifying glass. Once a day, look through it at something and then write down what you notice.

Like Blake, do you realize that you don't see "with" the eye but "through" it? It is a microscope, it is a telescope, according to your imagination.

97.

Fear a Height

Art is what remains of religion: the dance above the yawning abyss.

OCTAVIO PAZ

*H*ave you ever been tempted to leap from a deadly height?

The French call this impulse "l'appel du vide." The call of the void.

It's not about suicide, necessarily. In a study of this desire to jump, 50 percent of the participants not prone to killing themselves still felt tempted by the abyss.

One scientist thinks this "high place phenomenon" arises from the brain's misreading of a message sent from the body's self-preservation circuitry. Sensing danger—"You're too close to the ledge!"—the amygdala screams to the prefrontal cortex: "Jerk away!" By the time your slower conscious mind processes the fear, it says, "I recoiled from the ledge; that must mean I wanted to *jump*."

Another researcher theorizes that the desire to leap signals a tendency to roll the dice in the face of danger. You look over the ledge, terror floods your body; how can you feel safe? *Get to the ground*. Your mind briefly entertains the irrational belief that risking the jump might be safer than quivering on the precipice.

But philosopher Gary Cox maintains that longing to leap is more than neurons. It is "the vertigo of possibility. . . . The void seems to beckon us down, but really it is our own freedom . . . the very fact that we can always choose to go down the quick way."

Go to the top of your roof, or climb a tall tree, or open a high window, or travel to a cliff.

Push as close to the edge as safety allows. Look down.

Ask the abyss: Where in my life do I feel confined?

Once you have your answer, inquire: What can I do, no matter how extreme, to free myself?

Remain on the ledge for ten minutes, contemplating the question. Hopefully, in hovering over emptiness, you will fling your mind into new possibilities.

At the end of your time, climb back down, carefully.

Under the category "Elevation Meditation," list three adjectives that describe how you felt when looking over the ledge.

Repeat the exercise whenever you feel overly moored.

98.

Author Your Own Lexicon

[A]nd for several years, my Lexicon—was my only companion.

EMILY DICKINSON

Shakespeare invented some 1,700 words. He reveled in anthimeria (turning nouns to verbs, verbs to adjectives), portmanteaus (pressing two words into one, like "glare" and "gaze" into "glaze"), attaching prefixes and suffixes, and neologisms (made-up words), such as "lonely" and "elbow."

One source of this fecundity was Shakespeare's historical moment. The poet lived when English dictionaries and grammars were scarce, and the lack of rules invited innovation. The poet also composed in iambic pentameter, and so needed five stresses and ten syllables for each line; if an existing word didn't flow into the music, why not conjure a new one?

Historical context aside, Shakespeare did what all original writers do: make words for feelings not yet named. This can be a political act. The rules of language support cultural hierarchies: those in power dictate what one can say or can't. Writers fighting oppression articulate the silenced emotions. Expressing the unsaid sometimes requires new words.

Toni Morrison in *Beloved* creates "rememory"—a blend of "re-member" and "memory"—to describe a former slave's way of telling her stories; Sethe recovers parts of her traumatic past that the official histories—white histories—try to erase, and she weaves the pieces into meaningful, durable narratives.

Create your own new words. You can be serious, focusing on pains you've not been able to name, or whimsical, evoking harm-less eccentricities.

Write out the definition of a feeling there is no name for. For instance, "the act of wisping your fingers over the crevice your arm makes opposite the elbow until you get goose bumps"; or "the helpless feeling just after you've accidentally but possibly on purpose said something to your spouse that you know will cause a terrible fight."

Now create a word that fits your definition. "Arelliate" for the first, perhaps, and for the second, "repunder."

After you invent your word and its meaning, you will be able to explain yourself to yourself and to others with more precision. Your peculiarity will flare, not to mention the impish pleasure of breaking the decrees of Webster.

Block out ten pages in your notebook and there record your new words and their meanings. Do this at least once a week. Call the section "My Lexicon." It is a guide to your inmost spirit. When you have filled these ten pages, remove them from this notebook and staple them to the front of a new one that you will devote solely to your personal dictionary. It will be the first of many volumes.

99.

Complete a Final Project

*Y*ou study at a school that follows a dream-based curriculum. Your science teacher assigns a year-end essay: prove that you are, right this minute, though you appear to be sedentary and stable, falling through infinite space. What will your first sentence be?

Acknowledgments

All books begin long before words appear on the page, and this one started back in 1988, my first night outside of the US, in Athens, Greece. I was twenty-one, and I was traveling with a group of fellow college students, and the guy occupying the bunk above mine, whom I'd only just met on the plane, reached a drachma over the bed with one hand, and then passed his other in front of the coin, and . . . it vanished. Then he pulled both hands out of my view. He had said nothing the entire time. This was my first weird experience of Phil Arnold, who has since become my deranged psychopomp to realms too outlandish for maps.

Phil isn't the only friend whose odd antics have stoked my imagination. During my many weeknight art sessions with painter Kevin Calhoun, I developed an amateurish series of slightly uncanny portraits of Johnny Cash and Kim Novak.

Many of the ideas informing these exercises arose during long conversations during long runs with Terry Price and Andy Lester-Niles. Talks with Joanna Ruocco and Amy Catanzano, my creative writing colleagues at Wake Forest University, have consistently rallied me into surrealistic hilarity. I have also benefited mightily from giddily neurotic conversations with filmmaker Joel Tauber, whose documentaries uncannily blend social justice and farce. I have also enjoyed conversations with Angus MacLachlan, another filmmaker, about art, mortality, and how ridiculous it all is. I appreciate the support of Jessica Richard, my chairperson at Wake

Forest, who miraculously combines snarky wit and abiding generosity.

I would like to thank my agent, Matt McGowan, of Frances Goldin, who helped me shape this book in its earliest stages. His advice throughout was sage, and the book simply would not exist without him. My publisher at Penguin, Meg Leder, deftly helped me transform a very idiosyncratic and sometimes arcane confession into exercises eager to speak to the wide world. I also appreciate the always spot-on edits of Meg's assistant, Annika Karody.

But the most powerful influences on this book come from home: my wife, Fielding, whose bizarre (and gentle) jokes at my expense are deep forms of love; and my daughter, Una, to whom this book is dedicated, who has, since she was a small girl, inspired a craziness so exuberant it can be called redemptive.

Resources

1. Create an Overview Effect

The best place to learn about the overview effect is Frank White's *The Overview Effect: Space Exploration and Human Evolution* (Boston: Houghton Mifflin, 1978). A recent scholarly essay on the phenomenon is David B. Yaden et al., "The Overview Effect: Awe and Self-Transcendent Experience in Space Flight," *Psychology of Consciousness: Theory, Research, and Practice* 3, no. 1 (2016), 1–11, https://doi.org/10.1037/cns0000086. The only source I located for Mitchell's famous quote on "global consciousness" is *People*'s interview with the former astronaut. See People Staff, "Edgar Mitchell's Strange Voyage," *People*, April 8, 1974, https://people.com/archive/edgar-mitchells-strange-voyage-vol-1-no-6/. Two very informative magazine articles were essential for this entry: Jordan Rosenfield's "Scientists Are Trying to Find the Mystery of Awe," *The Cut*, May 26, 2016, https://www.thecut.com/2016/05/scientists-are-trying-to-solve-the-mystery-of-awe.html; and Olivia Goldhill's "Astronauts Report an 'Overview Effect' from the Awe of Space Travel—and You Can Replicate It Here on Earth," *Quartz*, September 6, 2016, https://qz.com/496201/astronauts-report-an-overview-effect-from-the-awe-of-space-travel-and-you-can-replicate-it-here-on-earth.

2. Encourage Moments of Yūgen

I draw my definition of yūgen from two of Alan Watts's works: "The Way of Tea, Part 2," *Alan Watts Organization*, https://alanwatts.org/3-6-4-the-way-of-tea-part-2; and a recorded lecture, "Alan Watts—The Feeling of Yūgen," YouTube video, 10:29, posted by Om, March 26, 2016, https://www.youtube.com/watch?v=rziSQ7jH1vQ. Even though Watts doesn't directly discuss yūgen in *The Way of Zen* (New York: Vintage, 1999), the book is a brilliant manual for how to experience the mood.

3. Astonish Your Words

William Styron's memoir *Darkness Visible: A Memoir of Madness* (New York: Random House, 1990) remains a devastating account of depression and healing. His quotation on the inadequacy of the word "depression" can be found on page 5. Several books on writing informed this exercise: Annie Dillard's *The Writing Life* (New York: Harper-Collins, 1989), John Gardner's *Art of Fiction: Notes on Craft for Young Writers* (New York: Vintage, 1991), Brian Dillon's *Essayism: On Form, Feeling, and Nonfiction* (New York: New York Review Books, 2018), and Mary Ruefle's *Madness, Rack, and Honey: Collected Lectures* (New York: Wave, 2012).

4. Turn This Book into a Shovel

The quote from Escher comes from his 1953 lecture, "On Being a Graphic Artist," http://web.archive.org/web/20030519205127/http://slesse.ca/cg/Escher.pdf. Imagining the number of uses for a paper clip has become a standard exercise in so-called creativity tests, designed to measure one's capacity for "divergent" thinking. Children, it turns out, score much higher on this test than adults. At kindergarten age, 98 percent of children score at the level of "genius" on the test. By the age of ten, only about half reach the genius level; by adulthood, only about 2 percent achieve this status. Children's minds are more pliable, flexible, open to possibility, while those of adults fix themselves in habits that promise predictability and control. For accounts of this decline in creative thinking, see the definitive book by Ken Robinson, *Out of Our Minds: Learning to Be Creative* (New York: Capstone, 2011) and Robinson's TED Talk: "Changing Education Paradigms," TED: Ideas Worth Spreading, October 2010, video, 11:40, https://www.ted.com/talks/sir_ken_robinson_changing_education_paradigms. See also Kamran Abbasi, "A Riot of Divergent Thinking," *Journal of the Royal Society of Medicine* 104, no. 10 (October 2011), 391, https://doi.org/10.1258/jrsm.2011.11k038. For more on the Zen master and the fan, see Francis H. Cook's *Sounds of Valley Streams: Enlightenment in Dōgen's Zen Translation of Nine Essays of Shobogenzo* (Albany: State University of New York Press, 1988).

5. Go Sinister

For more on Peirce, see Joseph Brent, *Charles Sanders Peirce: A Biography* (Bloomington: Indiana University Press, 1998); and Louis Menand, *The Metaphysical Club: A Story of Ideas in America* (New York: Farrar, Straus and Giroux, 2002).

6. Assemble a Shadow Box

For this entry, I have drawn from Deborah Solomon's *Utopia Parkway: The Life and Work of Joseph Cornell* (New York: Other Press, 2015); Charles Simic's *Dimestore Alchemy: The Art of Joseph Cornell* (New York: New York Review of Books, 2011); and Maggie Nelson's *Bluets* (Seattle, WA: Wave Books, 2009). Cornell's quote on his idea of "complete happiness" comes from his diary, July 10, 1948. You can access the entry on the website of the Archives of American Art, https://www.aaa.si.edu/collections/items/detail/joseph-cornell-diary-entry-16646. I found the quotation in Solomon, 123.

7. Arrange a Wunderkammer

Excellent introductions to different kinds of Wunderkammeren are Arallyn Primm, "11 Wonderful Wunderkammer, or Curiosity Cabinets," *Mental Floss*, March 5, 2014, https://www.mentalfloss.com/article/55324/11-wonderful-wunderkammer-or-curiosity-cabinets; and Caroline Mokrohajská, "What Is a Wunderkammer? Best Cabinets of Curiosities," *Daily Art Magazine*, July 6, 2020, https://www.dailyartmagazine.com/cabinets-of-curiosities. A good general introduction to Kircher's Wunderkammer is Laurel Byrnes, "Athanasius Kircher's Cabinet of Wonder: The Man Who Believed in Everything and His Museum of the Miraculous, Universal, and Absurd," *Biodiversity Heritage Library Blog*, June 6, 2019, https://blog.biodiversitylibrary.org/2019/06/athanasius-kirchers-cabinet-of-wonder.html. A useful scholarly exploration of Kircher is Paula Findlen, ed., *Athanasius Kircher: The Last Man Who Knew Everything* (New York: Routledge, 2004). Also see John Glassie's *A Man of Misconceptions: The Life of an Eccentric in an Age of Change* (New York: Riverhead, 2012). For more information on Mesa-Bain, see

Lucian Gomoll, "The Performative Spirit of Amalia Mesa-Bain's New World Wunderkammer," *Cultural Dynamics* 27, no. 3 (2015), 357–77, https://doi.org/10.1177/0921374015610130; Marianne K. McGrath, "An Interview with Amalia Mesa-Bains," *Art Insights*, April 30, 2021, https://nationalwca.org/amalia-mesa-bains; and Maximilíano Durón, "How to Altar the World: Amalia Mesa-Bain's Art Shifts the Way We See Art History," *ARTnews*, March 27, 2018, https://www.artnews.com /artnews/news/icons-amalia-mesa-bains-9988. The quotations from Mesa-Bain on loss and displacement can be found on Rachel Elizabeth Jones's blog (http://rachelelizabethjones.com/altar-la2/2015/7/17/2g4 fim9v76fv6656217a41g6ndn2id), where Jones interviews the artist. The interview was posted on July 21, 2015.

8. Design a Mappa Mundi

A fine introduction to the Mappa Mundi, with images, is Jerry Broton's "A History of the World in Twelve Maps: From Ptolemy to Google Earth, the World Has Been Mapped by Visionaries," *Time*, November 15, 2013, https://ideas.time.com/2013/11/21/a-history-of-the-world-in -twelve-maps/slide/claudius-ptolemy-world-map-150ad. For a scholarly introduction to al-Sharīf al-Idrīsī's map, see S. Maqbul Ahmad, "Cartography of al-Sharīf al-Idrīsī," in *The History of Cartography, Volume 2, Book 1: Cartography in the Traditional Islamic and South Asian Societies*, edited by J. B. Harley and D. Woodward (Chicago: University of Chicago Press, 1992), 156–72. A helpful look at al-Sharīf al-Idrīsī's map in the context of other maps of the world can be found in Macolm Forbes's "The Meaning of Maps: What the Arab World Used to Think the Globe Looked Like," *The National*, October 10, 2019, https://www .thenationalnews.com/arts-culture/art/the-meaning-of-maps-what -the-arab-world-used-to-think-the-globe-looked-like-1.921739. For general introductions to the Hereford Mappa Mundi, see "Exploring the Monstrous Other in Hereford's Mappa Mundi," on the blog *Medieval Monsters in the Hereford Mappa Mundi*, April 5, 2018, https://mappamundi monsters.wordpress.com/, and "The Hereford Mappamundi," on the website myoldmaps.com, http://www.myoldmaps.com/early-medieval -monographs/2261-ibn-fadi-allah-al/226-the-hereford-mappamundi

/226-hereford.pdf, accessed November 9, 2021. A scholarly account of the Hereford Mappa Mundi is P. D. A. Harvey's *The Hereford World Map* (Toronto: University of Toronto Press, 1996). A lucid study of sea monsters on medieval maps is Chet Van Duzer's *Sea Monsters on Medieval and Renaissance Maps* (London: British Library Publishing, 2013).

9. Forge a New Identity

Scientists call a proper name's shaping power the "Dorian Gray Effect." Just as the protagonist in Oscar Wilde's novel alters his portrait with his deeds, so our names shape our identities. In experiments supporting the theory, college-age students were able to match faces with names up to 40 percent of the time, while a computer did the same up to 64 percent of the time. See Yonat Zwebner, Anne-Laurier Sellier, Nir Rosenfield, and Jacob Goldenberg, "We Look Like Our Names: The Manifestation of Name Stereotypes in Facial Appearance," *Journal of Personality and Social Psychology* 112, no. 4 (2017), 527–54, https://doi.org/10.1037/pspa0000076.

10. Pursue Astral Pareidolia

A good article on the latest research in pareidolia and neurology is Lachlan Gilbert's "Why the Brain Is Programmed to See Faces in Everyday Objects," University of New South Wales Newsroom, August 14, 2020, https://newsroom.unsw.edu.au/news/science-tech/why-brain-programmed-see-faces-everyday-objects. Gilbert is reporting on the research of Colin Palmer and Colin Clifford, scientists at the University of New South Wales. They published their results in *Psychological Science* 31, no. 8 (2020), 1003–12, https://doi.org/10.1177/0956797620924814, under the title "Face Pareidolia Recruits Mechanisms for Detecting Human Social Attention." Palmer and Clifford focus on the role of pareidolia in evolution. Liu-Fang Zhou and Ming Meng are more interested in how different groups experience pareidolia in different ways. For instance, people with positive attitudes seem more prone to pareidolia, but lonely people are quite susceptible as well. Women experience pareidolia more than men. See Zhou and Meng's "Do You See the

'Face?': Individual Differences in Face Pareidolia," *Journal of Pacific Rim Psychology* 14, no. 2 (2020), 1–8, https://doi.org/10.1017/prp.2019.27.

11. Construct a Curvilinear Terrarium

The first quotation, on the brain's strong response to curved shapes, is from The Week Staff, "Do Our Brains Find Some Shapes More Beautiful Than Others," *The Week*, January 8, 2015, https://theweek.com /articles/456162/brains-find-some-shapes-more-beautiful-than -others. The second, on the pleasure the brain takes in convex shapes, is from the same article; it is a quote from a display card in an exhibition staged at the AAAS Art Gallery in Washington, DC, called "Beauty and the Brain Revealed." The exhibition reflects the joint work of Zanvyl Krieger Mind/Brain Institute, connected to Johns Hopkins, and Walters Art Museum, located in Baltimore.

12. Contrive a Shrine for Colors

For this exercise, I am most indebted to Maggie Nelson's *Bluets*, which I referenced earlier in relation to Joseph Cornell. Three other books that lyrically invoke the color are William H. Gass's *On Being Blue: A Philosophical Inquiry*, intro. Michael Gorra (New York: New York Review of Books Classics, 2014); Michel Pastoureau, *Blue: The History of a Color* (Princeton, NJ: Princeton University Press, 2018); and Alexander Theroux's *Primary Colors: Three Essays* (New York: Henry Holt, 1994).

13. Quest for Your Daemon

Phillip Pullman reveals his daemon in an interview with Lisa O'Kelly: "Philip Pullman: My Daemon Is a Raven, a Bird That Steals Things," *The Guardian*, September 22, 2017, https://www.theguardian.com/books /2017/oct/22/philip-pullman-my-daemon-is-a-raven-la-belle-sauvage -interview-questions. Tryee Daye's lines appear in "From Which I Flew," from his collection *Cardinal* (Port Townsend, WA: Copper Canyon Press, 2020). Dorianne Laux's "Bird" can be found in her *Awake* (Pittsburgh, PA: Carnegie Mellon Press, 1990). The lines from Louise

Bogan are from "Statues and Birds," contained in *The Blue Estuaries, Poems, 1923–1968* (New York: Farrar, Straus and Giroux, 1968). The two poems of Bashō can be found in *Bashō's Haiku: Selected Poems of Matsuo Bashō*, trans. and intro. David Landis Barnhill (Albany: State University of New York Press, 2004).

14. Quiver a Witch Stick

For more on dowsing, see George Applegate, *The Complete Book of Dowsing: The Definitive Guide to Finding Underground Water* (London: Element Books, 1998); and Christopher Bird, *The Divining Hand: The 500-Year-Old Mystery of Dowsing* (Atglen, PA: Schiffer Books, 2000).

15. Drink Air

Arthur Sze's poem "Transpirations" can be found in the *New Yorker* of April 13, 2020. It is the last poem of his most recent collection, *The Glass Constellation: New and Collected Poems* (Port Townsend, WA: Copper Canyon Press, 2021).

16. Novelize a Thrift Store

See Jennifer Baumgartner, "The Psychology of Vintage: An Interview with Bianca Turetsky, Author of *The Time-Traveling Fashionista*," *Psychology Today*, March 27, 2012, https://www.psychologytoday.com/gb /blog/the-psychology-dress/201203/the-psychology-vintage. Also see Turetsky's book *The Time-Traveling Fashionista on Board the Titanic (The Time-Traveling Fashionista 1)* (New York: Poppy, 2012). In the second and third volume of her series on vintage clothing, Turetsky explores, respectively, the fashion of Marie Antoinette and that of Cleopatra.

17. Transform Trash into Art

Joel Schwartzberg's article "The Psychology of Garage Sales," *HuffPost*, December 6, 2017, https://www.huffpost.com/entry/the-psychology-of -garage_b_112661, helped me think about the feelings connected with garage sales, as did Jason Feirman's "Garage Sale Tactics," *Psychology Today*, July 1, 2005, https://www.psychologytoday.com/us/articles /200507/garage-sale-tactics. Although he writes about flea markets instead of garage sales, Michael Rips' *The Golden Flea: A Story of Obsession and Collecting* (New York: Norton, 2021) is an entertaining meditation on trash and treasure.

18. Haunt Your Haunts

These lines come from Book 1 of Wordsworth's book-length poetic memoir, *The Prelude*. In her two great novels *To the Lighthouse* and *Mrs. Dalloway*, Virginia Woolf explores intense reminisces as "moments of being," instants that retain a strange luminousness long after they've passed and that perpetually electrify our lives.

19. Rearrange Your Childhood Bedroom

Literature about the power of rooms: E. M. Forster, *A Room with a View* (1908); Virginia Woolf, "A Room of One's Own" (1929); Gaston Bachelard, *The Poetics of Space* (1958); Annie Dillard, *The Writing Life* (1989); Maya Angelou, Interview with George Plimpton in *The Paris Review*'s The Art of Fiction, no. 119 (1990); and Emma Donohue, *Room* (2010).

20. Celebrate the Uninteresting Stuff

The book in which Perec recorded his details is called *An Attempt at Exhausting a Place in Paris*, trans. Marc Lowenthal (Cambridge, MA: Wakefield Press, 2010). By exploring the virtues of what we normally call "boredom," Perec's book exemplifies the primary argument of Michael Flaherty's *A Watched Pot: How We Experience Time* (New York: New York University Press, 2000): a "'boring' situation can present one with potentially engrossing circumstances" and actually heighten attention. Perec's experiment also connects with recent work on boredom and creativity. A recent study showed how people who went through a boring experience—sorting beans—later performed better on a creativity test than those who completed an art project. In her book *The Upside of Downtime* (New York: Robinson, 2017), psychologist Sandi Mann accounts for this result: boredom is "a search for neural stimulation that isn't satisfied. If we can't find that, our mind will create it."

21. Get a Zero

Two helpful scholarly books on Zen emptiness are Jay L. Garfield's translation of and commentary on Nagarjuna, *The Fundamental Wisdom of the Middle Way: Nagarjuna's Mulamadhyamakakarika* (Oxford: Oxford University Press, 1995); and C. W. Huntington and Geshe Namgyai Wangchen's translation of and commentary on Chandrakirti, *The Emptiness of Emptiness: An Introduction to Early Indian Madhyamika* (Honolulu: University of Hawaii Press, 1989). Also see Geshe Tashi Tsering's *Emptiness: The Foundations of Buddhist Thought*, vol. 1, ed. Gordon McDougall, foreword Lama Thubten Rinpoche (Somerville, MA: Wisdom, 2009).

22. Alienate Yourself from Yourself

I got the idea for this entry after reading Tom McClelland's "What Is It Like to Be John Malkovich," *The Postgraduate Journal of Aesthetics* 7, no. 2 (2010), 10–25, https://philpapers.org/rec/MCCWII-2. McClelland wonders if we can ever really know what it is like to be someone else. A useful concept in this regard is "qualia," illustrated famously by Frank Jackson's parable of Mary (which appears in his essay "What Did Mary Know?" *Journal of Philosophy* 83, no. 5 [May 1986], 291–95, and is invoked in an important moment in Alex Garland's *Ex Machina*). Imagine an expert in the study of vision named Mary. She is confined to a black-and-white room, from which she takes in the world through a black-and-white television monitor. She spends her time learning about the neurophysiology of color, to the point that there is nothing about perceiving the color blue that she doesn't know. When she is released one day and gets to experience blue for herself, will she learn anything new about the color? Yes. She will learn "what it is like" to experience blue. This feeling of "what-it-is-likeness" is called "qualia." But though we all know what it is like to experience blue, can we know what it is like to be Mary experiencing blue? Thomas Nagel answers this question in his famous essay, "What Is It Like to Be a Bat?" (*Philosophical Review* 83, no. 4 [October 1974], 435–50). He argues that we can imagine what it is like for a human to be a bat—we can picture ourselves flying, utilizing sonar, eating bugs—but we can't know what it is like for a bat to be bat, for then we would actually have to be a bat and would no longer be a human wanting to know what it is like to be a bat being a bat. To be simultaneously in a state of "what-it-is-like-to-be-a-bat" and a state of "being a bat" is impossible, unless you meet a witch in a forest.

23. Memorize a Poem Peripatetically

This quote from Brad Leithauser is from his January 25, 2013, essay in *The New Yorker*, "Why We Should Memorize."

24. Comb Plato's Beard

Quine's take on Plato's beard can be found in his essay "On What There Is," *Review of Metaphysics* 2 (1948/49), 21–38.

25. Irritate a Narcissist

This will be your very modest, fleeting effort to be a public artist, in the tradition of Banksy and Bambi, Plastic Jesus and Robin Rhode. For how the mirror has been used in contemporary art, see Tori Campbell, "Upon Reflection: The Mirror in Contemporary Art," *Artland*, https://magazine.artland.com/upon-reflection-the-mirror-in-contemporary-art/.

26. Listen to the Glass Wizard

Two unsettling poems in which the speaker is a mirror are Sylvia Plath's "Mirror"—written in 1961, published posthumously in *Crossing the Water* (1971)—and Elizabeth Bishop's "To Be Written on the Mirror in Whitewash"—written in 1937, published posthumously in *Poems* (2011).

27. Snort a Quarto

The quote on how books smell is from Matija Strlič et al., "Material Degradomics: On the Smell of Old Books," *Analytical Chemistry* 81, no. 20 (2009), 8617, https://doi.org/10.1021/ac9016049. I found the reference in Matt Soniak, "What Causes 'Old Book Smell'?" *Mental Floss*, July 19, 2012, https://www.mentalfloss.com/article/31235/what-causes-old-book-smell.

28. Fabricate a Story That Has Never Existed Before

The Salmon Rushdie quote on randomness comes from his essay "In Good Faith," *Newsweek*, February 12, 1990, 52.

29. Review Books That Do Not Exist

For more on Stanislaw Lem, see Paul Grimstead, "The Beautiful Mind-bending of Stanislaw Lem," *New Yorker*, January 6, 2019, https://www.newyorker.com/culture/culture-desk/the-beautiful-mind-bending-of-stanislaw-lem.

30. Imagine Your Life as a Peculiar Novel Written by a Lazy God

This exercise was inspired by Marc Forster's film *Stranger Than Fiction* (2006), about a character in a novel, played by Will Ferrell, trying to convince the author, Emma Thompson, not to kill him off. Other films about interactions between author and character are *Ruby Sparks* (2012) and *The Truman Show* (1998).

31. Crank Some Microfilm

A fine introduction to John Benjamin Dancer's life and work is Roy Winsby's "Micscape Hall of Fame: John Benjamin Dancer," first published in the newsletter of the Manchester Microscopical Society, no. 15, then reprinted on the website *Micscape: Exploring the Miniature World*, http://www.microscopy-uk.org.uk/index.html?http://www .microscopy-uk.org.uk/amateurs/qmc/hero1.html. See also L. L. Ardern's *John Benjamin Dancer: Instrument Maker, Optician, and the Originator of Microphotography* (London: Library Association, 1960). I was introduced to René Dragon in Ernie Smith's compelling piece in *Atlas Obscura*, "The Strange History of Microfilm, Which Will Be with Us for Centuries," June 20, 2016, https://www.atlasobscura.com/articles/the -strange-history-of-microfilm-which-will-be-with-us-for-centuries. More good information on Dragon can be found in Patricia C. Franks, ed., *The Handbook of Archival Practice* (Lanham, MD: Rowman and Littlefield, 2021), 198–201. The website of the FBI houses a detailed description of the hollow nickel affair. See "Hollow Nickel / Rudolph Abel," under "Famous Cases and Criminals," in the "History" section, https://www.fbi.gov/history/famous-cases/hollow-nickel-rudolph -abel. Craig Saper writes beautifully about the value of historical context in microfilm. See his "Microfilm Lasts Half a Millennium," *The Atlantic*, July 22, 2018, https://www.theatlantic.com/technology/archive /2018/07/microfilm-lasts-half-a-millennium/565643/.

32. Welcome the Earworm

The scientific article exploring the causes of earworms is Kelly Jakubowski, Sebastion Finkel, Lauren Stewart, and Daniel Müllensiefen, "Dissecting an Earworm: Melodic Features and Song Popularity Predict Involuntary Musical Imagery," *Psychology of Aesthetics, Creativity, and the Arts* 11, no. 2 (2017), 122–35, https://doi.org/10.1037 /aca0000090.

33. Conceive a Curse Word

The study of the power of profanity to ease the pain of the hand in ice water is Richard Stephens and Olly Roberts, "Swearing as a Response to Pain: Assessing Hypoalgesic Effects of 'Novel' Swear Words," *Frontiers in Psychology*, April 30, 2020, https://doi.org/10.3389/fpsyg.2020.00723. For an overview of research on the benefits of cursing, see Beth Ellwood,

"Repeating the 'F' Word Can Improve Threshold for Pain during an Ice Water Challenge," *PsyPost*, May 21, 2020, https://www.psypost.org /2020/05/repeating-the-f-word-can-improve-threshold-for-pain -during-an-ice-water-challenge-56828. There are many websites listing weird slang words, but the best source by far for the lyricism of profanity is Jonathon Green's *Green's Dictionary of Slang*, now available online: https://greensdictofslang.com. Also check out Green's Twitter feed, where he goes by @MisterSlang and daily posts gems of slang.

34. Hatch an Aphorism

The best source on the nuances of aphorism is Andrew Hui's *A Theory of Aphorism: From Confucius to Twitter* (Princeton, NJ: Princeton University Press, 2020). Hui, in an interview with Nigel Warburton on the website *Five Books*, recommends his favorite books of aphorisms and tells why he likes them. See "The Best Books on Aphorisms. Recommended by Andrew Hui," *Five Books*, https://fivebooks.com/best-books/aphorisms -andrew-hui. For a fine essay on aphorism and poetry, see Sharon Dolin, "Making Space for Aphorism: Exploring the Intersection between Aphorism and Poetry," *Poets.org*, September 12, 2011, https://poets.org/text /making-space-aphorism-exploring-intersection-between-aphorism -and-poetry.

35. Conjure Your Own Medieval Monster

A fantastic overview of the monsters of the European Middle Ages is Damien Kempf and Maria L. Gilbert's *Medieval Monsters* (London: British Library, 2015).

36. Chinwag with Your Evil Twin

For the research behind the likelihood of having a double, see Teghan Lewis and Maciej Henneberg, "Are Human Faces Unique? A Metric Approach to Finding Single Individuals without Duplicates in Large Samples," *Forensic Science Institute* 257 (December 2015), 514e1–e6, https:// doi.org/10.1016/j.forsciint.2015.09.003. A helpful analysis of this article, along with other pertinent research on the possibility of having a double, can be found in Zaria Gorvette, "You Are Surprisingly Likely to Have a Doppelgänger," *BBC Future*, July 13, 2016, https://www.bbc.com/future/article/20160712-you-are-surprisingly-likely-to-have-a-living-doppelganger.

37. Dress Your Döppelganger

The Cool Hour, "an international online destination for the creative cool," features a clothing line called Evil Twin, a fashion brand The Cool Hour admires "for its rebellious styles and edgy flare." The Australian clothing line offers "cool dress styles," "grungy shorts," "rad pants," and "80's inspired tops that will keep you hot and ready for the streets."

38. Journey to the Uncanny Valley

Masahiro Mori articulates his theory in "The Uncanny Valley," first published in 1970 and recently translated into English for the first time in *IEEE Spectrum*, June 12, 2012, https://spectrum.ieee.org/the-uncanny-valley. Jasia Reichardt explored the idea in her 1978 *Robots: Fact, Fiction, and Prediction* (New York: Penguin).

39. Consider a Victorian Doll

A fantastic book on the psychology of dolls, puppets, and cyborgs is Victoria Nelson's *The Secret Life of Puppets* (Harvard, MA: Harvard University Press, 2003).

40. Pass to Narnia

To make her 1988 sculpture *Closet*, Rachel Whiteread found a wardrobe that reminded her of her childhood, stripped the interior, and filled it with plaster. Once the plaster cured, she pulled off the wooden exterior and covered the mass in black felt. Her inspiration for the piece was her habit as a child of "sitting at the bottom of [her] parents' wardrobe, hiding among the shoes and clothes, and the smell and the blackness and the little chinks of light." I came across this quote in Imogen Racz's study of the psychology of interior spaces, *Art and the Home: Comfort, Alienation, and the Everyday* (London: Bloomsbury, 2015). Racz also cites Gaston Bachelard's 1958 evocation of the wardrobe's privacy: the closet is "[an] intimate space, space that is not open to just anybody." See Bachelard's *The Poetics of Space*, trans. Maria Joles, intro. Richard Kearney, foreword Mark Danielewski (New York: Penguin, 2012).

41. Get from A to Z

This entry was inspired by an unpublished manuscript by Philip Kuberski called *The A/Z Codex*. It explored the inner lives of Achilles and the Tortoise and it was way too weird (and good) to get published. See Kuberski's brilliant book on Stanley Kubrick, *Kubrick's Total Cinema: Philosophical Themes and Formal Qualities* (New York: Bloomsbury, 2014), and his exquisite essays on time, *The Persistence of Memory: Organism, Myth, Text* (Berkeley: University of California Press, 1993).

42. Sacralize the Absurd

Camus's "The Myth of Sisyphus" is perhaps the most provocative (and lyrical) philosophical study of the absurd gap between what we want and what we get. But the essay lacks the comic verve that the absurd deserves. More profound meditations on the condition are humorous. Think of the films of Buster Keaton, the music of Bob Dylan, Sarah Silverman's stand-up, the cinema of Miranda July.

43. Do Nothing

For an analysis on the value of doing nothing, see Tim Burkett's *Nothing Holy about It: The Zen of Being Just Who You Are*, foreword Norman Fischer (Boulder, CO: Shambhala, 2015). An excellent Western take on the value of doing nothing is Brian O'Conner's *Idleness: A Philosophical Essay* (Princeton, NJ: Princeton University Press, 2018).

44. Turn Off the Sound

This exercise was inspired by a "(Soma)tic poetry ritual" of poet and essayist CAConrad. Over three days, watch a favorite film with the sound turned off. The first day, focus on how art is depicted in the film; the second day, study nature in the movie; the third, examine the windows. Utilize binoculars and a magnifying glass when needed and record impressions in a notebook. Has the film not become a trilogy? You can find this exercise on the website for Woodland Pattern Book Center (https://woodlandpattern.org/project/trilogy). You can find other such rituals on CAConrad's blog, https://caconrad.blogspot.com, and in CAConrad's book *While Standing in Line with Death* (Seattle, WA: Wave Books, 2017).

45. List Your Top Five Weird Actors

Then there are actors who play a similar role every time, and are thus somewhat predictable, but nonetheless remain strange and compelling: from the old days, Cary Grant, Humphrey Bogart, Myrna Loy, Ingrid Bergman; from more recent times, Denzel Washington and Matt Damon, Diane Keaton and Halle Berry.

46. Cop a Deadpan

Steve Middlehurst's essay on the "deadpan aesthetic" in contemporary photography is a helpful introduction to the role of deadpan in performance. See "The Deadpan Aesthetic," on the blog *Steve Middlehurst Context and Narrative*, https://stevemiddlehurstcontextand narrative.wordpress.com/2015/02/24/the-deadpan-aesthetic.

47. Watch Strangers Watch You

In "The Expert's Guide to People Watching," Susan Kraus Whitbourne gives an overview of recent research on the psychology of people watching and offers advice on what to glean from the practice. The article can be found in *Psychology Today*, April 18, 2015, https://www.psychology

today.com/us/blog/fulfillment-any-age/201504/the-experts-guide
people watching.

48. Perform Dorian

See Giovanni B. Caputo et al., "Visual Perception during Mirror-Gazing at One's Own Face in Patients with Depression," *Scientific World Journal* (November 20, 2014), https://doi.org/10.1155/2014/946851.

49. Stare at Someone for a Long Time

See Giovanni B. Caputo, "Dissociation and Hallucination in Dyads Engaged through Interpersonal Staring," *Psychiatry Research* 228, no. 3 (August 2015), 659–63, https://doi.org/10.1016/j.psychres.2015.04.050.

50. Visit an Abandoned Building

Tim Edensor makes these remarks in an essay by Joann Greco, "The Psychology of Ruin Porn," *Bloomberg CityLab*, January 6, 2012, https://www.bloomberg.com/news/articles/2012-01-06/the-psychology-of-ruin-porn.

51. Pen Obituaries

For an overview on the memento mori theme in ancient Rome, see Peter Jones, *Memento Mori: What the Romans Can Tell Us about Old Age and Death* (London: Atlantic, 2020). Also see Paul Koudounaris, *The Empire of Death: A Cultural History of Ossuaries and Charnel Houses* (London: Thames and Hudson, 2011).

52. Rub a Tombstone

Keith Eggener's *Cemeteries* (New York: Norton, 2010) is a definitive history of burial practices. His book has been turned into an amusing narrated cartoon on *TEDEd* called "The Fascinating History of Cemeteries," https://ed.ted.com/lessons/the-fascinating-history-of-cemeteries-keith-eggener.

53. Doodle Around Your Grief

There are many books on the power of art to heal grief. Two I found useful are Sandra L. Bertman, *Grief and the Healing Arts: Creativity as Therapy* (New York: Routledge, 1999); and Barbara E. Thompson and Robert A. Neimeyer, eds., *Grief and the Expressive Arts: Practices for Creating Meaning* (New York: Routledge, 2014).

54. Explore Your Dark Corners

The inspiration for this exercise is a passage in Annie Dillard's *Holy the Firm*, rev. ed. (New York: Harper Perennial, 1998): "There is a spider in the bathroom with whom I keep a sort of company. Her little outfit always reminds me of a certain moth I helped to kill. The spider herself is of uncertain lineage, bulbous at the abdomen and drab. Her six-inch mess of a web works, works somehow, works miraculously, to keep her alive and me amazed. The web itself is in a corner behind the toilet, connecting tile wall to tile wall and floor, in a place where there is, I would have thought, scant traffic. Yet under the web are sixteen or so corpses she has tossed to the floor. The corpses appear to be mostly sow bugs, those little armadillo creatures who live to travel flat out in houses, and die round. There is also a new shred of earwig, three old spider skins, crinkled and clenched, and two moth bodies, wingless and huge and empty, moth bodies I drop to my knees to see."

55. Suspend a Pomander

A fine introduction to the importance of pomanders during European plagues appears on *Thorn and Thread*, the blog of Tiffan Fairamay (Sylvan Thorncraft). The piece is called "Warding Off Plague and Other Miasma with Pomanders," and it was posted on July 7, 2018 (https://thornandthread.wordpress.com/2018/07/07/warding-off-plague-and-other-miasma-with-pomanders). See also Paul Freedman's *Out of the East: Spices and Medieval Imagination* (New Haven, CT: Yale University Press, 2008).

56. Attend Your High Drone

First-rate overviews of research on why we tend to dislike recordings of our own voices are Neel Bhatt, "Why Do We Hate the Sound of Our Own Voices?" *The Conversation*, May 17, 2021, https://theconversation.com/why-do-we-hate-the-sound-of-our-own-voices-158376; and Philip Jaekl, "The Real Reason the Sound of Your Voice Makes You Cringe," *The Guardian*, July 12, 2018, https://www.theguardian.com/science/2018/jul/12/the-real-reason-the-sound-of-your-own-voice-makes-you-cringe. For a more scientific account of the phenomenon, see M. Lee, M. Drinnan, and P. Carding, "The Reliability and Validity of Patient Self-Rating of their Own Voice Quality," *Clinical Otolaryngology*, July 15, 2005, https://onlinelibrary.wiley.com/doi/10.1111/j.1365-2273.2005.01022.x.

57. Drop Pennies to Wake Yourself Up

Michelle Carr provides an overview of the relationship between hypnagogia and creativity in "How to Dream Like Salvador Dali," *Psychology Today*, February 20, 2015, https://www.psychologytoday.com/us/blog/dream-factory/201502/how-dream-salvador-dali. See also Jennifer Dorfman, Victor A. Shames, and John F. Kihlstrom, "Intuition, Incubation, and Insight: Implicit Cognition in Problem Solving," in *Implicit Cognition*, edited by G. D. M. Underwood (Oxford: Oxford University Press, 1996), 257–96; and Tore Nielsen, "A Self-Observational Study of Spontaneous Hypnagogic Imagery Using the Upright Napping Procedure," *Imagination, Cognition and Personality* 11, no. 4 (1992), https://doi.org/10.2190/3LVV-L5GY-UR5V-N0TG.

58. Decide If You Are Asleep or Awake

The inspiration behind this entry is the Hindu idea that Vishnu dreams the universe. But what if, one might ask, the Vishnu dreaming the universe is part of the dream of another Vishnu dreaming a universe that contains the first Vishnu dreaming the universe. And so on.

59. Scry

A picture of the object is here: https://wellcomecollection.org/works
/ryc4v9u9. The standard biography of Dee is Glyn Parry, *The Arch Conjurer of England: John Dee* (New Haven, CT: Yale University Press, 2014).

60. Cast a Magic Circle

For the earliest known uses of the magic circle, see Sam Mirelman,
"Mesopotamian Magic in Text and Performance," *Mesopotamian Medicine and Magic*, edited by Strahil V. Panayotov and Luděk Vacín
(Leiden: Brill, 2018). A practical guide for circle casting, from a Wiccan point of view, is Scott Cunningham, *Wicca: A Guide for the Solitary
Practitioner* (Woodbury, MN: Llewellyn, 1989). A Wiccan YouTube
video describes the rationale behind the magic circle: https://www.you
tube.com/watch?v=k-dFvnaVxoA.

61. Cut Your Own Tarot Deck

For two excellent brief histories of the tarot deck, see Hunter Oatman-
Stanford, "Tarot Mythology: The Surprising Origins of the World's Most
Misunderstood Cards," *Collectors Weekly*, June 18, 2014, https://www
.collectorsweekly.com/articles/the-surprising-origins-of-tarot-most
-misunderstood-cards; and Ferren Gipson, "Artmatters Podcast: Demys-
tifying Tarot Art," *Artmatters Podcast*, March 10, 2020, https://artuk.org
/discover/stories/art-matters-podcast-demystifying-tarot-art. A fabulous
book on how to use the cards is Rachel Pollack's *Seventy-Eight Degrees of
Wisdom: A Book of Tarot* (Newbury Port, MA: Weiser Books, 2007).

62. Master Legerdemain

An overview of the research on magic-based therapy is Richard Wise-
man and Caroline Watt, "Achieving the Impossible: A Review of Magic-
Based Interventions and Their Effects on Well-Being," *PeerJ* 6, e608,
https://doi.org/10.7717/peerj.6081. Richard Pitchford's quote appears
in the article.

63. Eat Spheroids

An overview of the research on round food and flavor is Paula Mejia, "The Power of Circles in Food and Drink," *Atlas Obscura*, January 18, 2018. Also see M. T. Fairhurst, D. Pritchard, D. Ospina, et al., "Bouba-Kiki in the Plate: Combining Crossmodal Correspondences to Change Flavour Experience," *Flavour* 4, no. 22 (2015), https://doi.org/10.1186/s13411-015-0032-2.

64. Fancy a Nook

The quote from Baudelaire appears in his poem "La Chevelure." It is a translation of the French "parnasse fecund," which could also be rendered as "fruitful" or "fecund" laziness. For a useful summary of recent research on creativity and daydreaming, see Barbara Field, "5 Positive Effects of Daydreaming," *Very Well Mind*, June 29, 2021, https://www.verywellmind.com/positives-about-daydreaming-5119107. A key scientific article on the subject is B. Baird et al., "Inspired by Distraction: Mind Wandering Facilitates Creative Incubation," *Psychological Science* 23, no. 10 (2012), 1117–22, https://doi:10.1177/0956797612446024.

65. Carve Soap

For informative introductions to ASMR, see German Lopez, "ASMR, Explained: Why Millions of People Are Watching YouTube Videos of Someone Whispering," *Vox*, May 25, 2018, https://www.vox.com/2015/7/15/8965393/asmr-video-youtube-autonomous-sensory-meridian-response; and Allison Mooney and Jason Klein, "ASMR Videos Are the Biggest YouTube Trend You've Never Heard Of," *Think with Google*, September 2016, https://www.thinkwithgoogle.com/consumer-insights/consumer-trends/asmr-videos-youtube-trend. A scientific article on ASMR is Emma L. Barratt and Nick J. Davis, "Autonomous Sensory Meridian Response (ASMR): A Flow-Like Mental State," *PeerJ* 3: e851, https://doi.org/10.7717/peerj.851. Here is a forty-five-minute ASMR YouTube video of soap carving: https://www.youtube.com/watch?v=orD6yIilRoA.

66. Mix Your Own Color

A detailed account of the discovery of paint in the Blombos Cave is Jonathan Amos, "Ancient 'Paint Factory' Unearthed," *BBC*, October 13, 2011, https://www.bbc.com/news/science-environment-15257259. The history of Tyrian purple can be found in Colin Schultz, "In Ancient Rome, Purple Dye Was Made from Snails," *Smithsonian Magazine*, October 10, 2013, https://www.smithsonianmag.com/smart-news/in-ancient-rome-purple-dye-was-made-from-snails-1239931. Mummy brown is examined in Philip McCouat, "The Life and Death of Mummy Brown," *Journal of Art in Society*, http://www.artinsociety.com/the-life-and-death-of-mummy-brown.html. For a history of yellow paint, see Kelly Grovier, "The Murky History of the Colour Yellow," *BBC*, September 6, 2016, https://www.bbc.com/culture/article/20180906-did-animal-cruelty-create-indian-yellow.

67. Make Ink

A brief, informative history of ink is Lydia Pine, "A History of Ink in Six Objects," *History Today*, May 16, 2018, https://www.historytoday.com/history-matters/history-ink-six-objects. For another handy history of ink, see "History of Pen and Ink," *History of Pencils*, accessed November 11, 2021, http://www.historyofpencils.com/writing-instruments-history/history-of-ink-and-pen/. If you want to learn all there is about ink and aren't afraid of prose from 1860, and if you like books with lovely print, check out Thaddeus Davids, *The History of Ink, Including Its Etymology, Chemistry, and Bibliography* (New York: Thaddeus Davids, 1860).

68. Inscribe Your Own Runes

The definitive book on runes and divination is Ralph H. Blum, *The Book of Runes*, 25th anniversary edition (New York: Thomas Dunne Books, 2008).

69. Dream a Game of Surrealism

Two excellent introductions to Dadaism and surrealism are Matthew Gale, *Dada and Surrealism A & I* (London: Phaidon, 1997); and David

Hopkins, *Dada and Surrealism: A Very Short Introduction* (Oxford: Oxford University Press, 2004).

70. Lay Off

"Let us treat the men and women well: treat them as if they were real; perhaps they are." —Emerson, "Experience"

71. Save a Nihilist

Like in the Coen brothers film *The Big Lebowski*, many philosophers don't take nihilism seriously, mainly because of the paradoxes in which the worldview finds itself. For instance, if I believe that there is no universal truth giving meaning and purpose to the world, then my claim that there is no universal truth—which aspires to be a universal truth—is rendered invalid.

72. Press Phosphene into Being

For an introduction to phosphene, see Liesl Goecker, "Why We See Swirling Colors When Our Eyes Are Closed," *The Swaddle*, August 2, 2019, https://theswaddle.com/seeing-colors-when-eyes-closed-phosphenes.

73. Hear Your Own Ears

George Foy's quote and his account of his experience at Orfield Laboratories can be found in his essay "Experience: I've Been to the Quietest Place on Earth," *The Guardian*, May 18, 2012, https://www.theguardian.com/lifeandstyle/2012/may/18/experience-quietest-place-on-earth. An overview of the science behind our inability to achieve total silence is Bryan Gardiner, "Big Question: Why Can Silence Make You Hear Things That Aren't There?" *Wired*, May 19, 2015, https://www.wired.com/2015/05/big-question-can-silence-make-hear-things-arent. For the sounds from space, see Ryan Whitwam, "NASA Reveals Eerie Whistling Electron Waves from Space," *ExtremeTech,* July 18, 2017, https://www.extremetech.com/extreme/252589-nasa-reveals-eerie-whistling-electron-waves-space; and Michelle Starr, "The Song of the Earth Is Like a Space

Whale," *CNet*, September 18, 2012, https://www.cnet.com/news/the-song
-of-the-earth-is-like-a-space-whale/.

74. Taxonomize Silence

For the poetry of taxonomy, in the context of the discovery of a red lantern jellyfish, see Jessica Benko, "Poetry and Taxonomy," *The World*, September 1, 2011, https://www.pri.org/stories/2011-09-01/poetry-and
-taxonomy. A wonderful poem on taxonomizing emotions is Nancy Ready's "Taxonomy," *Poets & Writers*, accessed August 18, 2021, https://www.pw.org/content/taxonomy. A poem on how taxonomy can be used for a racist tool is Evie Shockley's "Topsy's Notes on Taxonomy," *Literary Hub*, June 10, 2015, https://lithub.com/topsys-notes-on-taxonomy.

75. Anatomize Something

Recent literary anatomies are Chloe Benjamin's *The Anatomy of Dreams* (2014), Adam Gopnik's "Anatomy of Endings" (2014), and Norman Cousins' *An Anatomy of an Illness* (1979). A famous twentieth-century effort is Northrop Frye's *Anatomy of Criticism* (1957).

76. Identify with Your Hydrogen

An entertaining list of strange facts about the body's temporality is Brian Clegg's "20 Amazing Facts about the Human Body," *The Guardian*, January 26, 2013, https://www.theguardian.com/science/2013/jan
/27/20-human-body-facts-science. For an account of how particles constitute our identities, see Ali Sundermier, "The Particle Physics of You," *Symmetry*, March 11, 2015, https://www.symmetrymagazine.org/article
/the-particle-physics-of-you.

77. Distort Time

Robert Stolorow's quote on how trauma alters time is from his essay "Trauma Destroys Time," *Psychology Today*, October 21, 2015, https://www.psychologytoday.com/us/blog/feeling-relating-existing/201510
/trauma-destroys-time.

78. Collect Toadstools

A major source of this information on mushrooms is Lawrence Millman's *Fungipedia: A Brief Compendium of Mushroom Lore*, illus. Amy Jean Porter (Princeton, NJ: Princeton University Press, 2019). The quote from David W. Rose also comes from this volume, an excerpt from which you can find on *Literary Hub*, "The Cultural Encyclopedia of Mushrooms We Need Right Now," October 29, 2019, https://lithub .com/the-cultural-encyclopedia-of-mushrooms-that-we-need-right-now.

79. Kick Over a Log

Marty Calabrese models the physical qualities (versus the psychological ones) of this activity very nicely on his YouTube channel. See "Life Under a Log! Nature Challenge #7," April 17, 2020, https://www.youtube .com/watch?v=2GXCNtkYfRc.

80. Sniff Play-Doh

Alan Hirsch, director of the Smell and Taste Treatment and Research Foundation, discusses the psychology of odor in an NPR interview with Sacha Pfeiffer: "The Swaying Power of Scented Spaces Isn't Always Right Under Our Noses," NPR, August 10, 2019, https://www.npr .org/transcripts/750012448.

81. Look Up

See Fred H. Previc, "The Role of Extrapersonal Brain Spaces in Religious Activity," *Conscious Cognition* 15, no. 3 (September 2006), 500–39, https://psycnet.apa.org/doi/10.1016/j.concog.2005.09.009.

82. Build a Model of Your Foot

An excellent introduction to votive-making and healing is Carly Silver, "Why Ancient Greek Temples Were Full of Disembodied Clay Limbs," *Atlas Obscura*, March 3, 2017, https://www.atlasobscura.com /articles/greek-temples-clay-limbs. The Wellcome Collection in London has posted an informative video on votives on YouTube: "Votive Offerings: How Were They Used to Treat Illness?" Wellcome Collection, April 30, 2020, video 40, https://www.youtube.com/watch?v=Uh9MnA6bRzI.

83. Seed a Wasteland

For an overview of how "urban wastelands" might foster biodiversity, see Juliane Mathey and Peter Rink, "Urban Wastelands—A Chance for Biodiversity in Cities? Ecological Aspects, Social Perceptions and Acceptance of Wilderness by Residents," in *Urban Biodiversity and Design*, edited by Norbert Müller, P. Werner, and J. G. Kelcey (Hoboken, NJ: Wiley-Blackwell, 2010).

84. Compose Your Own *Atlas Obscura*

For Kircher's influence on the creators of the website, see John Seabrook, "Kooky! Dept: Wonder Boys: Athanasius Kircher Society," *New Yorker*, January 21, 2007, https://www.newyorker.com/magazine/2007/01/29/kooky-dept-wonder-boys. In the article, Seabrook describes the inaugural meeting of the Kircher Society. The program featured lectures by Anthony Grafton, an esteemed scholar of the Renaissance; Kim Peek, mnemonic phenom and model for Dustin Hoffman's Rain Man; Rosamond Purcell, a historian of science who showed slides of Kircher's curiosities; and Colonel Joe Kittinger, who in 1960 parachuted 102,800 feet—a record. The evening concluded with Foer mounting the podium with a two-foot-long walrus penis bone, known as a baculum. He announced that the person with the words "Walrus Baculum" on his program would get this prize. A man in the audience leapt up. "All right!" Foer exclaimed, and he raised the bone over his head.

85. Speak "Takete"

For an introduction to what is known as the "bouba / kiki" phenomenon, see Pete Etchells, "The Bouba / Kiki Effect: How Do We Link Shapes to Sounds?" *The Guardian*, October 17, 2016, https://www.the guardian.com/science/head-quarters/2016/oct/17/the-boubakiki -effect-how-do-we-link-shapes-to-sounds.

86. Form a Word That *Is* What It Means

The quote on good writing becoming thing-like is from *Journals and Miscellaneous Notebooks of Ralph Waldo Emerson, Volume III, 1826–1832*, eds. William H. Gilman and Alfred R. Ferguson (Cambridge, MA: Belknap Press of Harvard University Press, 1963), 271. The quote on sonnets and conchs can be found in the essay "The Poet."

87. Paint Stones

Over the past five years, people have been placing painted rocks in yards as acts of kindness. The rocks are called "kindness rocks." For more on the phenomenon, see Terri Peters, "Kindness Rocks! How Rock Painting Is Connecting Families Nationwide," *USA Today*, May 24, 2017, https://www.today.com/parents/rock-painting-groups-connect -families-communities-t111934. The rocks encouraged by this exercise should be "weirdness rocks."

88. Be a Prophet

"We too must write Bibles." —Emerson, "Goethe; or, The Writer"

89. Swerve

Philosopher of science Michel Serres extends Lucretius's cosmogeny to ethics in *The Birth of Physics*, first published in 1977. See also his *Hermes: Literature, Science, Philosophy* from 1983. Other works exploring how so-called chaos theory—the idea that all orders are dependent upon disorder and all turbulence contains pattern—can inform human behavior are Ilya Prigogine and Isabelle Stengers, *Order Out of Chaos: Man's New Dialogue with Nature* (1984) and Gary Zukav's *The Dancing Wu-Li Masters: An Overview of the New Physics* (1979).

90. Play the Flâneur

The quote from Susan Sontag is from her 1977 book *On Photography* (New York: Picador, 2001). Baudelaire's lines on kaleidoscopic consciousness can be found in an 1863 essay now published in *Painter of Modern*

Life (New York: Da Capo, 1964). Woolf's lines can be found in her 1930 essay "Street Haunting: A London Adventure," *Street Haunting (Pocket Penguin 70's)* (New York: Penguin Vintage Classics, 2005).

91. Take Your Turn

"He most honors my style who learns under it to destroy the teacher." —Walt Whitman, "Song of Myself"

92. Glance Askance

This quote is from Edward Emerson, "Henry Thoreau as Remembered by a Young Friend (1917)," *American Transcendentalist Web*, accessed August 15, 2021, https://archive.vcu.edu/english/engweb/transcendental ism/authors/thoreau/youngfriend.html.

93. Perform the Percy Switcheroo

Walker Percy's "Loss of Creature" can be found in his 1975 collection of essays, *The Message in the Bottle: How Queer Man Is, How Queer Language Is, and What One Has to Do with the Other* (New York: Picador, 2000), 119–49.

94. Spend a Day as a Termite

See Manny Farber, "White Elephant Art vs. Termite Art," *Film Culture* 27 (Winter 1962–3).

95. Frequent a Shoreline

For research on water proximity and happiness, see Zachary Slobig, "Mind Your Body: The Brain Aquatic," *Psychology Today*, July 1, 2014, https://www.psychologytoday.com/us/articles/201407/mind-your-body -the-brain-aquatic. For more on the "blue mind" effect, check out Wallace J. Nichols, *Blue Mind: The Surprising Science That Shows How Being Near, In, On, or Under Water Can Make You Happier, Healthier, More Well Connected, and Better at What You Do* (New York: Back Bay, 2015).

96. Manufacture a Portable Door

Others have connected the door to exuberant perception. Walt Whitman in "Song of Myself" (1855) urges readers to open to the suffering of others. How? "Unscrew the locks from the doors! / Unscrew the doors themselves from their jambs!" In *Doors of Perception* (1954), Aldous Huxley concludes that mescalin is a portal to the mesmerizing complexities of particular things, such as a playing card. Just as Huxley was completing his book, Allen Ginsberg was starting *Howl*, a celebration of countercultural misfits. His epigraph: Whitman's plea to break open the doors. Channeling these liberatory energies, Jim Morrison named his band The Doors.

97. Fear a Height

Jennifer L. Himes et al. make the argument that the urge to jump is a misreading of the urge to live. See "An Urge to Jump Affirms an Urge to Live: An Empirical Examination of the High Place Phenomenon," *Journal of Affective Disorders* 136, no. 3 (February 2012), 1114–20, https://doi.org/10.1016/j.jad.2011.10.005. As reported in Jessica Siegel, "You Feel the Urge to Jump: The Science and Philosophy of Looking Down from a High Place," *Nautilus*, March 30, 2017, https://nautil.us/issue/46/balance/why-you-feel-the-urge-to-jump, Adam Anderson has proposed the "roll the dice" theory: the idea that we feel the urge to jump because we think it's the quickest way to safety. Siegel also cites Gary Cox's *The Existentialist's Guide to Death, the Universe, and Nothingness* (New York: Continuum, 2012), where Cox, a philosopher, argues that the desire to jump express our love of freedom.

98. Author Your Own Lexicon

For more on Shakespeare's inventions of words, see David Crystal and Ben Crystal, *Shakespeare's Words: A Glossary and Language Companion,* pref. Stanley Wells (New York: Penguin, 2002). See also Josh Jones, "The 1700+ Words Invented by Shakespeare," *Open Culture*, April 2, 2018, https://www.openculture.com/2018/04/the-1700-words-invented-by-shakespeare.html; and Amanda Mabillard, "Words Shakespeare

Invented," Shakespeare Online, August 20, 2000, http://www.shake speare-online.com/biography/wordsinvented.html. For Toni Morrison's novel, see *Beloved* (New York: Knopf, 1987).

99. Complete a Final Project

The first sentence of James Joyce's *Finnegans Wake* (1939) is "riverrun, past Eve and Adam's, from swerve of shore to bend of bay, brings us by a commodius vicus of recirculation back to Howth Castle and Environs." But the sentence only makes sense when combined with the last line of the novel: "A lone a last a loved a long the." The full sentence, connecting beginning and end, is "A lone a last a loved a long the riverrun, past Eve and Adam's, from swerve of shore to bend of bay, brings us by a commodius vicus of recirculation back to Howth Castle and Environs." The effect is this: since you can only complete the final line by returning to the beginning of the book, once you start reading the *Wake*, you never stop. You endlessly fall into the narrative.